IN-HOUSE TEAM

Editor: Mike Toller

Features editor: Alexi Duggins

Senior editorial assistant: Joly B

Editorial and production assistan

Editorial assistance: Anton Tweedale, Claire Gardiner, Kelsey Strand-Polyak, Katy Georgiou

Designer: Sarah Winter

Design assistance: Caitlin Kenney, Sara Gramner

Picture research: Alex Amend

Production consultant: Iain Leslie

Web editor: Cameron J Macphail

National ad sales: Sue Ostler, Zee Ahmad

Local ad sales: Gemma Coldwell

Distribution: Nativeps

Financial controller: Sharon Evans

Managing director: Ian Merricks

Publisher: Itchy Group

© 2007 Itchy Group

ISBN: 978-1-905705-19-1

...rby, ...adford, ...eafield, ...larwood, Christina Tilott, Jane Ramsey, Olivia Midgley, Shelley O'Connor, Elle Ward

Photography: Hayley Proudfoot, Ross Williams Natalie Theobold, Tess Eaton, Mario Alberto Dorrottya Verses, Chris Grossmeier, Selma Yalazi Dawani, Tim Ireland

Illustrations: Tom Denbigh, Si Clark, Joly Braime

Cover illustration: Si Clark (www.si-clark.co.uk)

Itchy Group
White Horse Yard
78 Liverpool Road
London, N1 0QD
Tel: 020 7288 9810
Fax: 020 7288 9815
E-mail: editor@itchymedia.co.uk
Web: www.itchycity.co.uk

□□□□□□□□□□□

Welcome to Itchy 2007

You lucky thing, you. Whether you've bought, borrowed, begged or pinched it off your best mate's bookshelf, you've managed to get your mucky paddles on an Itchy guide. And what a guide it is. If you're a regular reader, you're probably already impressing your friends with your dazzling knowledge of where to head for a rip-roaring time. If, on the other hand, you're a trembling Itchy virgin, then get ready to live life as you've never lived it before. We've spent the last year scouring Leeds for the very best places to booze, cruise, schmooze, snooze and lose ourselves to the forces of pleasure. As ever, we've made the necessary, erm, sacrifices in the name of our research – dancing nights away, shopping 'til we flop and of course, eating and drinking more than we ever thought possible. But we're still alive, and now we're ready to do the whole lot again. Come with us if you're up for it – the first round's on us...

KEY TO SYMBOLS

◯ Opening times

⑪ Itchy's favourite dish

⊘ Cost of a bottle of house wine

⊕ Admission price

Welcome to Leeds

Now don't go thinking that this is some poncey guide that's going to give you the simple facts about a place. Oh no. If you want that then we don't want you putting your fingers between our covers. Itchy does things a bit differently. We go the extra mile, eating, drinking and dancing in every bar, pub, club and restaurant in the name of (ahem) research.

So, full of goodness and bursting at the seams with naughtiness, Itchy is your long-lost soul mate. We're the sidekick who has the skins, we're the compadre that knows the door staff and we're the buddy that has a friend who knows someone that can get us the best table in the house. After nine years of living it up we're still going strong, and we're still making sure that your time going out in Leeds is the wildest, tastiest and most eventful of your whole life.

In Newcastle you'll find the Geordies and in London there's the infamous Cock-er-neys, but in Leeds we have the best nickname of all… Loiners. With Loiners like comedy genius Julian Barratt, crazy indie kids Kaiser Chiefs and, of course, the ever popular Chris Moyles, it's about time the rest of the world started using this word too. That said, people are already aware of many of the virtues of this great city: Leeds Met gained an award in 2006 from *The Times Higher* for 'Outstanding Contributions to the Community'. Which probably means that they are constantly contributing to the drunken nightlife and, of course, the headwear placed upon the statues in front of The Old Post Office every September.

Itchy's mission is to bring you the very best of Leeds. We'll give you the skinny on new shops and where to find the hidden gems in the city's cluster of restaurants and bars. Like the new design lounge recently opened above the Victoria Quarter's Aqua, where the fashion perverts among you can pick up bespoke garments and fancy commissioned pieces of clothing. We'll also tell you about the city's latest makeovers and facelifts: The Calls Grill is now an Argentinian steak house called The River Plate, and if you've not been along to Normans in a while, get down, get in and get smooth with their new alpine look. Don't ever let Itchy leave your side, because without us, you'll end up fine dining at a popular finger food style restaurant where every meal begins with Mc or drinking pop in a sweaty club surrounded by your untrustworthy friends, Cazbo, Shazbo and Dazbo, all dressed in fake designer tat. Don't do it to yourself and don't do it to Leeds. Stick with us, live the dream Loiners and honorary Loiners alike, and live it good.

Introduction

Two hours in Leeds

So what's your excuse for only spending two hours here? On your way to Scotland from London? Got a bit of time to kill before a gig? Or is it that your folks are coming on a check-up visit and you want to keep them entertained? Whichever it is, here's Itchy's guide to filling in a couple of hours. First things first (obviously). You'll be as hungry as Jonny Vegas at a Miss Burger King contest, so we recommend simultaneously filling up and checking out some local artwork at Art's (42 Call Lane, 0113 243 8243). Once full and refreshed, suck in your belly and get some purchasing done. If you've got more money than sense, then take your big ol' gold over to the Knightsbridge of the North, aka Victoria Quarter (0113 245 5333) and blow it all. If not, take your horse and cart to the Corn Exchange, stopping at Blue Rinse (11 Call Lane, 0113 245 1735) on the way; you'll end up with ten times as much loot as all the other poncey fools you encounter. Don't forget to leave a little time before the end for a quick game of giant chess off Millennium Square near the Town Hall. What? You're leaving so soon? No phone number? Not even a hug…?

Two days in Leeds

It's nice to get away for a weekend, isn't it? Well, it is except for the fact that it's so bloody hard to fit all the great stuff that cities have to do into just two days of sightseeing. If only there were some sort of kindly soul out there good enough to tell you exactly what you should be getting up to with your time. Oh hang on a minute...

STAY – Set up your Leeds weekend HQ in style at 42 The Calls (er, 42 The Calls, 0113 244 0099) or for a home from home, pitch up in a serviced apartment in Residence6 (3 Infirmary Street, 0113 285 6250) or the brand new Roomzzz (2 Burley Road, 0113 233 0400).

SHOP – Go mad with your bank balance at Harvey Nic's (107–111 Briggate, 0113 204 8888). Begin your attack with bags and accessories then advance to the floors above for all-out warfare, with shoes and dresses as your allies. Rendezvous in the 4th Floor Restaurant to plan your final assault, before heading back to base with your plunder.

ACTIVITIES – If you're into big, bulky guys with odd-shaped balls or skinny guys with red balls then take a ten minute train or bus ride from the centre to Headingley, where you'll find yourself in the midst of the city's cricket and rugby grounds (and not any kind of strangely-testicled men, we're afraid). If you'd rather suck on a vet's glove than watch any kind of sports, indulge in some culture at Leeds City Art Gallery (The Headrow, 0113 247 8248).

EAT – For romancing in the city, nibble on some Euro cuisine at Plush (10 York Place, 0113 234 3344) to get things going or if you fancy something a bit more exotic, you could always go ahead and spoil yourself. Take a short taxi ride to Chapel Allerton and visit Sukhothai (8 Regent Street, 0113 237 0141) for the best Thai food that Leeds has to offer.

DRINK – Drinking in style takes place at Norman's (36 Call Lane, 0113 234 3988) and if you're in need of some 'alternative therapy', Dr Wu's (35 Call Lane, 0113 242 7629) offers treatment in the form of live bands and all that jazz.

CLUB – Carry on the 'real music' theme and mooch over to Wire (2–8 Call Lane, 0113 243 1481), or for something a lot more colourful and wild, shimmy into Fibre (168 Lower Briggate, 0870 120 0888) for some cheeky fun.

Eat

Eat

CAFÉS

Amigos

70 Abbey Road, Kirkstall
(0113) 228 3737

Arriba, arriba amigos. Roll on down to the bottom of the hill near Kirkstall Abbey and enter the house that's dressed like a Spanish café. This is a proper family-run tapas bar, offering genuinely brilliant food and genuinely brilliant service at mouthwatering prices. It's surrounded on all sides by sweet terraces that you would never want to live in for the very real fear of becoming an Amigos addict. The food is amazing, and with all the attention they lavish on you, this is one amigo you won't be saying 'adios' to in a hurry.

🕑 *Mon–Sat, 5.30pm–11pm*

Art's Café Bar and Restaurant

42 Call Lane
(0113) 243 8243

'Oh my Gaudi, Dali-ing, a Euro-Brit upmarket café with a gallery exhibiting local artists. We must Van Gogh, for Sunday brunch, lunch, or an evening meal; the quality food (with regional specialities from ice cream to Yorkshire feta) doesn't cost much Monet, so the Banksy manager's happy. I'll park my Botticelli on one seat; perch your Pic-ass-o on another, and we'll both get a free card for discounts and invites to special events. It's the dog's Pollocks.'

🕑 *Mon–Fri, 12pm–11pm; Sat, 12pm–2am; Sun, 10.30am–11pm*

🍴 *Ham hock with root veg, £12.50*

💷 *£11.95*

Bagel Nash

Leeds City Station
(0113) 241 6811

To Itchy, the idea of getting out of bed early to make a healthy breakfast scares the living daylights out of us, (indeed we refuse to believe that there's more than one 7 o'clock every day). Our trick is to stop at Bagel Nash on our way to work and pick up a scrumptiously good start to the day. On days when you're not working, you can even potter around and pick up a hobbitish spot of second-breakfast on which to masticate. And don't you snigger like you don't know what that word means. Honestly, we'd expect that humour from a *Zoo* reader, but not you.

🕑 *Mon–Fri, 7am–3.30pm*

🍴 *New Yorker bagel, £3*

Indie Joze Café Bar

16 York Place

(0113) 245 3192

If your Temples are Doomed with a banging headache, and the cupboards are bare, save a stale packet of pickled onion Space Raiders (of the Lost Ark), then make Indie Joze your first Crusade, not your Last. With a holy grail of a menu spanning cappuccinos, cocktails and sumptuous sarnies, all served to a funky soundtrack, this business district haven has been soothing the suits since '92 and is the absolute business for kicking back in. Available for hire, it's indie-mand for parties.

🕒 *Mon–Fri, 11am–11pm; Sat, 7pm–11pm; Food, Mon–Fri, 12pm–3pm*

🍴 *Jerk chicken French stick, £5.95*

💷 *£11.95*

Juice

The Courtyard Level, The Light

(0113) 244 9017

As far as we're concerned, juice is the only worthwhile way of hitting your five portions of fresh fruit and veg. Although apparently baked beans count, so maybe a Terry's Chocolate Orange does as well. Anyway, juicy, juicy, very juicy smoothies are the name of the game here, and if you haven't got time to pick up a real meal in the middle of your ten-minute lunch hour without giving yourself a stitch, then pop into this one-stop vitamin shop for a healthy and surprisingly filling alternative to your usual stomach-liner.

🕒 *Mon–Fri, 8am–6pm; Sat, 9am–6pm; Sun, 10am–5pm*

🍴 *Triple berry smoothie, £2.80*

Eat

LS6 Café Bar

16a Headingley Lane
(0113) 294 5464

We still sweetly remember this place under its old title, Clock, and have spent many an hour moulding the retro benches to the shape of our ample buttocks. After chowing too many monstro all day brekkies and Thai curries, our bums now have their own postcode – presumably why they changed the name to LS6. It still tick tocks all the boxes for a great spot to fill up: free papers, board games, an arty, friendly vibe, smashing smoothies (with alcoholic varieties), and a buzzing bar in the evening. A true Hyde Park beacon.

Mon–Sun, 11am–11pm

Havana sarnie, salad and coleslaw, £5

£9

Café Noir Pizzeria

4 Sovereign Place
(0113) 234 0788

This place is like the new intern in the office that we can't do without (seriously, you don't think we actually write these books ourselves?). They'll do absolutely anything you ask them, any time you like, without ever complaining. Breakfast baps, paninis, wraps, salads, pizza, pasta, burgers and mains, need we say more? Yes, because if we didn't mention the fact that all of this food tastes amazing too, it would eat us up inside and we'd never sleep happily ever after again. Noir even gives you the the option of ordering online, so get your money's worth and send that intern out to grab lunch for everyone in the office.

Mon–Sat, 9am 'til late

RESTAURANTS

Aire

32 The Calls

(0113) 245 5500

Looks good on paper but the reality disappoints. Its red-bricked, cavernous look, waterfront terrace and young, attractive clientele are all let down by the shabby entrance and furnishings that look like they've been lifted from a skip. Avoid the bangers and mash, but give the perfectly cooked and juicy steak a try. Also, be prepared for the food to take longer to arrive than a one-legged rambler with an old map.

🕙 *Mon–Sat, 11am–11pm;*
Sun, 12pm–10.30pm
🍴 *Homemade steak burger and chips, £5.25*
✅ *£8.75*

Bibis Criterion

Criterion Place

(0113) 243 0905

One for the *Footballers Wives* generation. Ostentatious décor reflects the opulence of this Italian paradise. Appearances count for everything, and ignoring the fact that Bibis is on the ground floor of a multi-storey car park, you'll still want a pizza the action. Despite the revolving-door style of filling and emptying tables, the food stands up to analysis, and the whole extravagance of the place overcomes all doubts in the end.

🕙 *Mon–Tue, 12pm–2pm & 6pm–11pm;*
Wed–Fri, 12pm–2pm & 6pm–11.30pm;
Sat, 12pm–2pm & 5.30pm–11.30pm;
Sun, 5.30pm–10.30pm
🍴 *Ravioli 'Villa Rosa', £10.50*
✅ *£13.25*

The Arc

19 Ash Road, Headingley

(0113) 275 2223

The students and young professionals went in two by two, hurrah, hurrah. The students and young professionals went in two by two, hurrah, hurrah. Everyone went in two by two, hurrah, there was no elephant nor kangaroo, and they all went into The Arc, for to get out of the rain. Thank God that's out of our system, and we'll quickly tell you that Arc boasts a swish, contemporary sort of appearance mixed with a wide, reasonably-priced menu of delicious food (mmm, delicious food) before you notice Arc's spelt different from how Noah spelt it.

🕙 *Mon–Sun, 12pm–10.45pm*
🍴 *Penne vodka, £7.25*
✅ *Mon–Thu, £6.95; Fri–Sat, £10.95*

Brasserie Forty 4

42–44 The Calls

(0113) 234 3232

Walk in and you are taken out of Leeds and dropped into the barn conversion that you dream of owning one day. Not the sort of place to go to if you're planning a night out on the piss and winning the jackpot on *Who Wants To Be An ASBOaire?*, but that's good news for those who are up for some smart casual dining with friends and a bit of celeb spotting. After all, if the food is good enough for professional sportsmen and TV 'stars' then it's good enough for us, right?

🕙 *Mon–Thu, 12pm–2pm & 6pm–10.30pm;*
Fri, 12pm–2pm & 6pm–11pm; Sat, 6pm–11pm
🍴 *Spinach gnocchi with ricotta cheese*
sauce and rocket salad, £12.50
✅ *£14.95*

Eat

Brett's Fish Restaurant

14 North Lane, Headingley

(0113) 232 3344

This sit-down and sit-up-straight, elbows-off-the-table posh chippy actually does an awesome full English, as well as fish and chips that could easily stand the criticism of anyone hailing from a British seaside town. Fuzz your way down one morning in a hung-over daze for some quality grease to get you feeling Brett and breezy again, ready for a bit of browsing round Headingley, before heading home for a nap. It's worth saving your post-club snack money and spending it in here instead.

Tue–Fri, 12pm–2pm & 5pm–9pm; Sat, 11.30am–9.30pm; Sun, 12pm–8pm

Large haddock and chips, 8.25

£8.95

Cactus Lounge

3 St Peters Square

(0113) 243 6553

Itchy initially read the sign for this place as 'Cactus Lunge', which sounds a bit like a *Street Fighter* special move, and so we were somewhat relieved to find that nobody was going to spring out at us with a spiky pot plant. Instead, ay caramba, they sprang towards us bearing hot, hot, hot enchiladas, followed by margaritas to smother the fire, both made exceedingly well and in portions meriting at least three Xs before the L. A far cry from plastic Tex Mex, you'd be a prick not to stride on over there.

Mon–Fri, 12pm–2pm & 5pm 'til late; Sat, 5pm 'til late

Fajitas, £11.95

£10.90

Browns Restaurant

70–72 The Headrow

(0113) 243 9353

Probably the kind of place you'd be better off going to for a laugh. Get pissed, order your food in the Queen's English and laugh your tits off as the waiter walks off in disgust. It's full of people pretending they're classier than they actually are (keeping up with the Joneses and all that) and any hint of enjoyment may result an exclusion order from the managment. The food is pretty, but nothing to get excited over. To be frank, daahling, Browns is as dull as its name. The new black it most certainly ain't.

Mon–Sat, 11am–11pm; Sun, 12pm–12.30am

Braised lamb shank, £13.50

£10.75

Café Guru

6 Brewery Place

(0113) 244 2255

Not the sort of guru who's old and sweaty and tries to convince girls that the path to enlightenment involves getting nuddie, but one that lets us stuff oursleves with beautiful curries and doesn't judge us for smothering absolutely everything with tasty mango chutney. The kind who'll point us in the direction of dishes we might be scared to try elsewhere. This place looks like Bollywood and smells like heaven. They don't make the hottest curry to impress your mates with how hard you are, but far more delicious.

🕒 *Mon–Sun, 6pm–11pm*

🍴 *Tikka masala, £7.50*

💰 *£10*

Casa Mia Grande

33–37 Harrogate Road, Chapel Allerton

(08704) 445 157

If Casa Mia was a man, he'd have slicked-back hair and use the chat-up line, 'Ey baby, woop woop, sexy lady ey'. And it would work. Does for Italian food what Il Divo think they're doing for pseudo-classical music (FYI boys, singing *Without You* in Italian doesn't make it classical). You'll be fed only the best pizza, pasta and desserts. But do expect to whack elbows with the next table, and have grown wrinkles deep enough to swim in by the time you get served.

🕒 *Mon–Thu, 12pm–2.30pm & 5.30pm–10.30pm; Fri–Sat, 12pm–2.30pm & 5.30pm–11pm; Sun, 12.30pm–9.30pm*

🍴 *Lasagne al forno, £7.95*

💰 *£13.45*

Caliente Café

53 Otley Road, Headingley

(0113) 2749841

This isn't just another number on the list of Mexican joints in Leeds. It tops the list of Mexican joints in Leeds. Don a moustache, pop a sombrero on your noggin, drink tequila and bash a piñata 'til the sun rises. Or, avoid such gross national stereotyping and just have a nice supper. Of course they offer the usual as far as our expectations of Mexican food go, but nevertheless it's the atmosphere and service that gives it top spot. In the midst of Uni Heights it's priced perfectly for its location. Students, the mother ship has landed.

🕒 *Wed–Sun, 6.30pm–10.30pm*

🍴 *Chorizo and black bean enfriolada and choice of drink, £10*

Chaophraya

20a Blayds Court

(0113) 244 9339

Owned by a twin whose sibling set up another fave of ours: Sukhothai (which is named after their birthplace). Apparently Chaophraya is a river that's traditionally thought of as the bloodline of the Thai people. You can be sure that when so much thought has gone into the name, everything else is going to be spectacular. The service is brilliant, so you won't be Thai'd up for long waiting for the amazing food. In fact, you might say that when it comes to deciding whether this place is better than its sister venue, it's a Thai for first place.

🕒 *Mon–Sun, 12pm–3pm & 5pm–11pm*

🍴 *Pad kratium prik tai, £7.49*

💰 *£8.95*

Eat

Chino Latino
Boar Lane
(0113) 380 4080

You've got a city job with your degree, joined a wanky gym and discovered non-Primark fashion. All you need now is somewhere to spend your 'I earn so much I could give it away' money. Throw it at Chino Latino in return for somewhere to eat, chill and listen to funky music. Then, when your pan-Asian meal arrives, prepared by an award-winning Japanese chef, be moved to tears by its exquisite taste, and forget yourself for just a moment, while you remember what real enjoyment is.

🕒 *Mon–Sat, 12pm–3pm & 6pm–10.30pm; Sun, 6pm–10pm*

🍴 *Duck with plum wine poached pears, £19*

💰 *£13*

Citrus
11 North Lane
(0113) 274 9002

Many venues aiming to ensnare students seem to promise a meal, pint, two shots and someone to go home with and catch mutant crotch critters from for about 25p. Fortunately, Citrus is too classy to pander to such demands, while still getting the uni vote every time. Gorgeous modern fusion food, affordable prices, a cool bar upstairs with a big screen and pool table for après-dinner chilling make for a jolly good evening. Plus, everyone knows citrus is packed with vitamin C, so it's healthy just being here.

🕒 *Mon–Fri, 9am–4.30pm & 5.30pm–10.30pm; Sat–Sun, 10.30am–4.30pm & 5.30pm–10.30pm*

🍴 *Feta and cherry tomato torte, £4.95*

💰 *£8.95/BYO (£2.50 corkage)*

The Courtyard
25–37 Cookridge Street
(0113) 203 1831

Leeds' party central (as it's known to anyone who's anyone) also does bloody good food. Every kind of bloody good food, at that. Outside under the fairy light sky in the Courtyard's courtyard, their summer BBQs are hugely popular with students and hedonists alike. But grilled meat and the perfect pub crawl starter are not all that this place has to offer. All the meats, fish and general snack food are to be found inside under the watchful eye of the big screen TV and sexy décor.

🕒 *Sun–Thu, 11.30am–12pm; Fri–Sat, 11.30am–1am*

🍴 *Chicken penne arrabiata, £3.95*

💰 *£6.95*

Cuban Heels

28–30 Assembly Street
(0113) 234 6115

Stashed away under the arches, this place is like a cosy cave, and fairly free of the fraggles that can frequent these cobbled streets. And it only takes about £25 to stuff yourself with South American style goodies and a full smokin' barrel of shooters. The grub here is gorgeous – well, the stuff on your plate, at least; we're less sure about the little pickled maggoty-type variant you might find festering at the bottom of your tequila glass. But never underestimate the heeling qualities of a sozzled worm.

🕐 *Mon–Thu, 12pm–9.30pm;*
Fri–Sat, 12pm–11.30pm
🍴 *Salt cod burrito, £10.95*
💲 *£8.95*

Dutch Pot

247 Chapeltown Road
(0113) 262 7280

'Pass de Dutch Pat fram de left hand sayde...' If the closest you've got to the Caribbean is doing the old 'beer-can' impression then shake out of it and get stuck into some seriously easygoing flavour. Well, it's more boom-shack-a-lacka than Bob Marley, but you get the idea, right? Phew, got the clichés out of the way then. It may be just a café, but it's one for regular outings in the 'international experiences' section of your places-to-go list. What? Everyone's making them nowadays. Shut up. Loser.

🕐 *Sun–Thu, 9am–10pm; Fri, 9am–12am;*
Sat, 11am–12am
🍴 *Curried goat, rice and peas, £4.15*

Dough Bistro

293 Spen Lane
(0113) 278 7255

A wise man once said that the most beautiful sound in the English language was 'BYO'. In your face, 'cellar door'. Inside this former bakery the décor is very New York. Yes, we said it, New York in old Yorkshire. Exposed bricks and everything else wood, it's cosy enough for a sweet little anniversary and understanding enough for a hard break-up. With all sorts of cuisine from monkfish to duck, and using as much seasonal produce as possible, this place puts the dough in dough-ray-me. Perhaps.

🕐 *Tue–Sat, 6pm–9.30pm*
🍴 *Beef fillet with wholegrain mustard and red wine sauce, £15.95*
💲 *BYO, no corkage charge*

Eat

Fairuz

Fairfax House, Merrion Street

(0113) 243 4923

Everyone loves Spanish tapas and Greek meze; Fairuz serves up the Lebanese take on moreish morsels and is perfect for those who can't settle on just one dish. Opt for the full-blown 'mazza' and get more dips than you'd need to delouse an army of sheep, enough salads and warm breads to feed crowds of Biblical proportions, and a gut-busting main menu to boot. Once a month, they lay on the full Lebanese experience with an all-you-can-eat buffet and sexy belly dancing. Seeing as you'll certainly have a belly by the time you leave, you may as well learn how to shake it in a not altogether unsightly way.

◉ *Tue–Sat, 5.30pm 'til late; Sun, 12pm–6pm*

Hansa Gujarati

72–74 North Street

(0113) 244 4408

Tired of guessing whether your curry contains soggy doggy, froggy, or moggy? Switch to Hansa's, a homely restaurant offering traditional vegetarian Gujarati cuisine; real home-cooked Indian rather than some hybridised version for English tastes. Mrs Hansa Dhabi's longstanding Leeds' favourite has recently had to loosen its own belt-buckles to make room for a multitude of awards; Itchy wonders if any of them were from the RSPCA. It's slightly pricey for food with no meat, but the taste is worth every last penny.

◉ *Mon–Sun, 6pm–10.30pm*
🍴 *Gujarati mixed veg curry, £6.25*
💰 *£11*

Fried and tested

Breakfast means something different for everyone, so here's the skinny on where to get it your way. Rock up to **Bagel Nash** (Leeds City Station, 0113 241 6811) for an amazing speedy treat of a bagel full of cream cheesy goodness. However, if you're coming up from a night of heavy Headingley hedonism, why not fill up on a full English at **Brett's** (14 North Lane, 0113 232 3344) to give your body the grease-hit that it craves. If you're playing at being a workaholic and have given up sitting down for meals, then **Whistle Stop** (Leeds City Station, 0113 245 3263) offers cereal packs and muesli with yoghurt or fresh fruit to take to work with you. If none of these can get your day off to a good start, you're probably beyond help anyway.

Harvey Nichols 4th Floor Restaurant

107–111 Briggate

(0113) 204 8000

Fine dining for the young and restless. After a productive day strolling around the store, you could be in danger of losing track of your belly's needs. Fear not: a leisurely glide up to the 4th floor provides you with culinary luxury as well as beautiful guys and dolls to serve you nibbles and Beaujolais as you recline. For a post-pay day posh treat, try the award winning Thornhill Dexter ribeye with a champagne cocktail at the bar for afters. Gastronomical decadence.

🕐 **Mon–Wed, 10am–5pm; Thu–Sat, 10am–10pm; Sun, 12pm–4pm**

🍴 **Roast breast of pheasant, £14**

💷 **£13.50**

Kadas

3 Crown Street

(0113) 243 3433

No matter what you eat before you go out, the munchies demon is guaranteed to stage a takeaway takeover of your innards at around 3am. If you've had enough of waking up with wheelie bin breath and a stomach full of more junk than a bring and buy sale, then shimmy over to late-night Morrocan-style café Kadas and flop into the huge cushions while you sink a toasted panini and a cup of coffee. A cosy end to an evening, and the end too of food greasier than Olivia Newton-John's spray-on trewsers.

🕐 **Sun–Mon, 11am–4am; Fri–Sat, 11am–5am**

🍴 **Chicken, hummus and cheese panini, £3.50**

💷 **BYO**

Jake's Bar and Grill

27 Call Lane

(0113) 243 1110

Be prepared to fork out a little more than your standard pay-eat-leave establishment, but if you manage to hole up in one of the snug candlelit mini-caverns in this basement beauty, you won't want to leave anyway. A skeleton was apparently found within the wall cavities when they first did up this hot-diggety dug-out, and Itchy can't think of a better final resting place. Perfect if you fancy a date with lots of eyebrow wiggling and innuendo; bag one of the little nooks at the back to gain some privacy while you work your magic over dessert.

🕐 **Mon–Sat, 5pm–2am**

🍴 **Fillet steak, £14.50 (Tue, £7.25)**

💷 **£12.50**

La Besi

211 Clarendon Road

(0113) 244 1177

Nestled away from the zombie-filled streets of Hyde Park lives a super sweet Italian, home of the best pizza in Leeds. The care that manager Bafti puts into looking after the customers is mirrored in the way that the chef looks after the food. It's hard to leave this beauty alone, especially with its BYO policy and an offy just a hop, skip, and an embarassing stumble-on-a-wonky-pavement-slab down the road. You'd be well-advised to become bezzie mates with the folks over at La Besi.

🕐 **Mon–Fri, 12pm–3pm & 5pm–10.30pm; Sat, 5pm–11.30pm**

🍴 **Tagliatelle with salmon and broccoli in a cream sauce, £6.95**

Eat

La Tasca

4 Russell Street
(0113) 244 2205

Wine, chat, eat, laugh, eat, wine, laugh, chat, eat tapas, hurrah. The only thing that will disappoint about eating here is the realisation that you have no beach to go to in the morning, no banana boat to bounce around on and no tan to come home with. Be careful over how many people you take here, 'cos the more there are the louder it will be, increasing the risk of your cheeks still aching the next morning from all the giggles. Inimitable cuisine combined with authentic Spanish décor and sexy staff whisks you away from Leeds for a night of Mediterranean pleasure.

Ⓒ *Mon–Sun, 12pm–11pm*
Ⓓ *£9.45*

Little Tokyo

24 Central Road
(0113) 243 9090

The pick 'n' mix of intriguing, pretty tidbits to wrap your chops and chopsticks round at this miniature wonder makes you look and feel like you've eaten and enjoyed Japanese food for your entire life. Helpful staff and an easy menu, as well as the huge selection of addictive bento boxes, will fast-forward your confidence to the point where you are willing to try just about anything. Itchy recommends a soundtrack of Phil Collins while you fill your face: 'suss-suss-sushi-o, woah!'

Ⓒ *Mon–Thu, 11.30am–10pm; Fri–Sat, 11.30am–11pm*
Ⓘ *Spare rib bento box, £11.99*
Ⓓ *£10.95*

Livebait Fish Restaurant

11–15 Wharf Street, The Calls

(0113) 244 4144

Food so great, there are even sly rumours that Itchy named ourselves after one of the dishes (we had crabs). Select seafood from a vast catch, fresher than any Bel Air prince and with a wider choice of delicacies than bed-hopping Hef has cotton-tailed partners. The atmosphere's friendly, service ef-fish-ient, and the platters – served on heaps of shaved ice – are to dive for. Prawn stars and sex cods, feel that lob-stirring in your loins – you've just found heaven.

🕒 *Mon–Thu, 12pm–3pm & 5pm–10.30pm; Fri–Sat, 12pm–3pm & 5pm–11pm*

🍴 *Sea bass and ginger chilli crab with baby spinach and noodles, £15.95*

💷 *£11.90*

Ma Potter's Restaurant

64 The Headrow

(0113) 246 1620

Ma Potter's may sound like it belongs in the middle of the countryside with the possibility of sneaking away from the watchful eye of the cute old lady owner without paying, but if you believe this you are in for a shock. When your tummy's rumbling for some no-fuss soul food, everybody knows that Ma comes to the rescue. Old age remedies such as paninis and burgers are injected into your system without causing your bank manager to have a fit when you end up asking for more of an overdraft.

🕒 *Mon–Sat, 10am–11pm; Sun, 10am–11pm*

🍴 *Chargrilled tuna, £10.95*

💷 *£11.55*

The Living Room

7 Greek Street

(0870) 44 22 720

My oh my, real food has never been delivered to us in such a pretty way. A comfortable restaurant with non-pretentious intentions, it delivers the kind of décor and atmosphere that's perfect for enjoying on all occasions. All the obvious choices for a European meal, but most importantly the food arrives without looking or tasting like it's been on a ten minute holiday to Ready-meal Island. Try one of their oven baked omelettes for brunch and you'll know exactly what we mean.

🕒 *Mon–Tue, 10am–12am; Wed–Thu, 10am–1am; Fri–Sat, 10am–2am; Sun, 11am–12am*

🍴 *Roasted smoked salmon fillet, £12.95*

💷 *£11.50*

Eat

The Mill Race

2–4 Commercial Road, Kirkstall

(0113) 275 7555

Gone are the days of eating out only to find that your chemically-enhanced food has been spoiled all the more by being over-baked and shriveled to within an inch of its tiny, sad, factory-grown life. Just a short taxi ride from the bars and clubs of Headingley, The Mill Race serves a mixture of international and British cuisine at very accessible prices, mostly made from locally-sourced produce. And by this we assume they don't mean they're shipped in straight from the local turkey twizzler factory.

🕒 *Tue–Sat, 5.30pm–11pm;*
Sun, 12pm–11pm
🍴 *2 course set menu, £10 (Tue–Fri)*
💷 *£10.95*

Nando's

Unit 4, The Light, The Headrow

(0113) 242 8908

Ok, so Nando's is a chain and there aren't many of those that can redeem themselves from the depths of prefab restaurant hell. That said, they've got a formula for a reason: it works. There's none of this waiting for your cola nonsense. No, it's do it yourself, as much as you want. You can choose how hot and spicy your food is, and you can make up for the healthy grilled chicken by eating loads of yummy chips and other Portuguese delicacies.

🕒 *Sun–Thu, 11am–11pm;*
Fri–Sat, 11am–12pm
🍴 *Peri-Peri whole chicken platter, chips and coleslaw, £15.25*
💷 *Bottomless soft drink, £1.70*

Mio Modo Restaurant, Bar and Gallery

2–4 Britannia Street

(0113) 242 6655

'This is the best and most exclusive restaurant in Yorkshire,' owner Ardi proclaims of Mia Modo. Woah there, we'll be the judge of that. Although, we will admit he has a point. It is seriously swanky, with neutral décor enhanced by shots of colour in all the right places, and the service is just posh enough for rough sorts like us. Mia Modo is the Audrey Hepburn of restaurants, stylish and stunning, with a beautiful heart and soul.

🕒 *Mon–Fri, 12pm–2.30pm & 6pm–10.30pm;*
Sat, 6pm–11pm
🍴 *Spaghetti carbonara, £6.95*
💷 *£11.50*

Nick's Brasserie

No 20 Dock Street

(0113) 246 9444

Anyone who has the balls to give their restaurant a name even remotely similar to Bev's Café, the greasy spoon on the corner, deserves a look. Nick's isn't a greasy spoon, nor is it a café, or in fact your good old town brasserie. No, Nick's is a contemporary take on all of the above, (well, except the greasy spoon of course). Good old seasonal food served by good old attentive staff, this is one of those special British restaurants we should all choose to savour.

🕒 *Sun–Thu, 12pm–10.30pm; Fri–Sat 12pm–11pm; Sun, 12pm–9.30pm*
🍴 *Chargrilled tuna steak, £12.50*
💷 *£9.50*

No 3 York Place

3 York Place

(0113) 245 9922

Get your new togs on, style your hair and overdo the accessories because we're dining in style today. The building oozes class from the inside out, the menu holds the key to certain happiness, and if you ever wanted to try oysters, this is the environment to do it in. If you want to prove to your parents that Leeds is a good place to be or show off to your mates, then take them here for a French fancying.

🕒 *Mon–Fri, 12pm–2pm & 6.30pm–10pm; Sat, 6.30pm–10pm*

🍴 *Braised shoulder of lamb, creamed savoy cabbage, celeriac puree, redcurrant and rosemary sauce, £12*

💰 *£14*

The Old Police Station

106 Harrogate Road

(0113) 266 8999

'Dear Ma, I'm not sorry for committing my crimes, 'cos being here is like heaven. They have dressed it up real nice. The wardens are very friendly and serve us our meals like in a top restaurant. The prison cook must be here on some sort of TV show deal 'cos his food is fit for a king and the top brass don't boss us about like at that last place. They always makes sure we are treated with respect. I don't ever want to leave this cop shop. Love, Jonny the Slayer. P.S. It's more like caviar than porridge.'

🕒 *Mon–Thu, 12pm–11pm; Fri–Sat, 12pm–12am; Sun, 12pm–10.30pm*

🍴 *Fixed two course dinner, £12*

💰 *£12*

Eat

Pasta Romagna

26 Albion Place
(0113) 245 1569

Beware – step over the threshold of this café and you will not be allowed to leave without eating. The staff appear to be suffering from Stockholm Syndrome under the rule of exuberant, opera-singing owner Mrs Walker, whose relentless belting out of the Italian greats once saw her threatened with a noise abatement order by the council. The killjoys seem to have backed off now; maybe they were topped with sauce and zapped in the microwave like a gremlin in front of your eyes, just like the pasta they serve. The pizza's a safer option.

🕑 *Mon–Sun, 8am–6pm*
🍴 *Pasta of the day, £5*
💳 *£9.95*

Quantro Restaurant

3 Royal Parade, Harrogate, North Yorkshire
(0113) 288 8063

It might be a forty-five minute drive from Leeds, but that's a small inconvenience. The menu reads like poetry, or a personal love letter from the chef, and will make you dream about ordering everything and taking it home to savour at your leisure. With a Savoy-trained head chef, the names of dishes may be a bit confusing for us mere mortals, but try the Monkfish & hot chilli squid, black ink taleteller and curried velouté, then dramatise the whole event to your mates afterwards.

🕑 *Mon–Sat, 12pm–2pm; Mon–Fri,*
6pm–10pm; Sat, 6pm–10.30pm
🍴 *Calves' liver with greens, roast baby onions & pancetta, fondant potato, £13.50*
💳 *£11.80*

Plush

10 York Place
(0113) 234 3344

Plush should employ Dirvla Kirwan to read the specials to diners in the style of her voiceover from the Marks and Sparks ads. There's something sensual about the menu here, and the delight in this food porn isn't limited to the dishes themselves. The ambient atmosphere and comfortable surroundings make it ideal for a little pre-bedroom action. Foreplay is feeding your partner the tempura king prawns, followed in a timely fashion by the orgy of game and seafood main courses on offer. Climax with the chocolate brioche pudding.

🕑 *Mon–Sat, 12pm–2.30pm & 6pm–10.30pm*
🍴 *Seafood linguine, £13.90*
💳 *£13.95*

The Restaurant Bar and Grill

The Old Post Office, 3 City Square
(0113) 244 9625

This is the new jar on the shelf of the sweet shop that is the Leeds dining experience, and it seems like everyone is clamouring to stick their grubby mitt in. Dominating City Square like the fresh sherbet in town, the Old Post Office shows off its new look at every opportunity and is styled for only the sharpest of our sexy city's food-loving clientele. You'll need to smash your piggy bank for this trip out, but it'll be worth all the pennies that heaven can spare.

🕑 *Mon–Fri, 7am–11pm;*
Sat–Sun, 9am–11pm
🍴 *Marinated breast of chicken with Malayan spices, £12.95*
💳 *£13.50*

Roots & Fruits

10 Grand Arcade

(0113) 242 8313

Cute as a button and helping to ensure that you can still do yours up, this place serves intensely healthy vegetarian grub that doesn't taste like it might have been recycled from the insides of bog rolls with a sprinkling of Trill. Gone are the days of the carnivores' mass sigh when their veggie mate wants to eat out; Roots & Fruits offer dishes that even meat-eaters can get excited about, and staff are friendly and welcoming to all, whether virtuously vegan or beefed-up and bloodthirsty. Don't be disappointed by the mumsy décor; the money saved on the refurb probably went on the ingredients.

🕒 *Mon–Fri, 11am–7pm; Sat, 10am–7pm*

Shabab

2 Eastgate

(0113) 246 8988

Not just your usual bodged together curry place, this is a deluxe Indian restaurant. They haven't scrimped on a thing and the décor gives the joint a palatial feel. Quite fittingly too, as you can expect to be treated like royalty by the wonderfully friendly and attentive staff. This place is so splendid it starts to remind you of that kid at school who was good at everything and popular and made you feel sick with jealousy. But suppress those feelings (they'll give you indigestion) and marvel at the wondrous food.

🕒 *Mon–Sun, 11.30am–2.30pm & 6pm–11.45pm*

🍴 *Chicken tikka masala, £6.50*

💲 *£10.90*

Sala Thai

13–17 Shaw Lane, Headingley

(0113) 278 8400

A good restaurant for a night out with new friends, the menu is simple and full of the usual but the atmosphere is fantastic; bound to become one of those regular affairs. Speaking of which, it's a good job they don't have an internet café tucked away in here – more than one of the Itchy crew's dads made reference to getting themselves a Thai bride online after being served by the waitresses in their traditional uniforms. Leave the old man at home; there's nothing like your father getting all stirred up in his tweed turn-ups to put you off your noodles.

🕒 *Mon–Sat, 6pm–10.30pm*

💲 *£8.50*

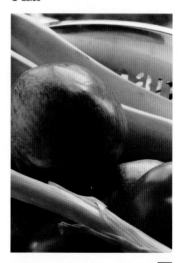

Eat

Sheesh Mahal

346–348 Kirkstall Road

(08452) 412 120

Old food may not be that great, but old recipes surely are the best. Noted as one of the best Indian restaurants in the area, Sheesh Mahal's owner Azram Chaudhry knows exactly how to treat his customers and feeds them recipes that have been passed down throughout his family. Highly rated by Leeds' Curry Club (we're so joining) and frequented by Jimmy Savile, it must have something jingly jangly special about it. If you're struggling to choose between this place and the generic-looking Indian/American across the road, don't even bother crossing.

🕒 *Mon–Sun, 5pm–12am*

🍴 *King prawn rogan josh, £6.70*

Shogun Teppanyaki

Granary Wharf, Canal Basin

(0113) 245 1856

As the sun set over the city of Leeds, the student asked his master how to give the people fright and delight, with the restaurant as his chosen weapon. And Shogun Teppanyaki was born. Fall in love with sushi and hotplate sizzlers, and indulge in a Shogun wedding; partner the kitchen with the table, add some flames and offensive food tools, and sit watching your dinner being created before your eyes. Expect the usual yet welcome suspects on the menu, and use the 'oh, look at that' trick to take a cheeky pinch from your fellows' plates.

🕒 *Mon–Sun, 12pm–2pm & 6pm–10.30pm*

🍴 *Set menu, £25*

💷 *£9.50*

Si Sushi

14 Electric Press, Great George Street

(08456) 445 055

Chopsticks at the ready, chop chop, for a quickfire round of Itchy's quiz, Jap-phrase. Soy what you see. What's this? Ah yes; sushi, soup, noodles, smoothies, sake, rice dishes and teas, all fresh as Magic Tree, to take away, have delivered, or eat in. And what is Mr Chops doing? Refurbing? So Si Sushi now has a more zesty modern Japanese feel, and can whip up breakfast with a twist from 7am? And cocktails? That's right! You've won Phil Collins' excellent new single, *Su-su-sushio*.

🕒 *Mon–Wed, 7am–11pm; Thu–Fri, 7am–late; Sat, 12pm–late; Sun, 12pm–10pm*

🍴 *Spicy chicken noodle soup, £6.50*

💷 *£13.95*

Simply Heathcotes

Canal Wharf, Water Lane

(0113) 244 6611

Pop on tha fla' cap 'n gatha up tha friends 'n potter on daahn ta enjoy seriously scrooomptious scran. This is Yorkshire this is, but we're not all stuck in t' past, no. We might not be reet posh but we know t' difference 'tween what looks good and what looks shabby. 'N that's what we like 'bout Simply Heathcotes. It's a smart place to get fed 'n watered, 'n t' scran tastes gran'. Don tha best togs for this aahtin'.

🕑 *Mon–Sat, 12pm–2.30pm; Mon–Fri, 6pm–10pm; Sat 6pm–11pm; Sun, 12pm–9pm*

🍴 *Pan fried sea bass with black olive linguine, grilled artichokes and rosemary, £15.50*

💰 *£13.95*

Suburban Style Bar & Bistro

5 Stainbeck Lane, Chapel Allerton

(0113) 237 4374

If you're wanting a night out that doesn't involve drinking competitions and dressing up as superheroes, then venture away from Headingley and the City Centre, to the thoroughly more grown up Suburban Style Bistro in Chapel Allerton. With its mix of classic-style eatery and contemporary bar, this place is perfect for a chilled night. Order some generous sized portions of goats' cheese bruschetta and mouth-watering sea bass and finish off with a liqueur coffee. It's time to embrace suburbia.

🕑 *Tue–Sat, 5.30pm 'til late*

🍴 *Deep fried brie followed by gourmet sausage and mash, £10*

💰 *£9.95*

Sous Le Nez En Ville

9 Quebec Street

(0113) 244 0108

If you're trying to impress that sexy bit you've been trying to get your teeth into for weeks, take them here. It's pricey enough to make you look like you're doing them a favour, and the atmosphere could get even the most sparkling Rainbow Brite to kiss a skanky Garbage Pail Kid. Authentic food, a rustic environment and attentive staff make it (and you) a winner. Expect an evening of polite conversation giving way to oh la la. And if you're lucky, a la la la la lum, a la la la la lum lum le lum lum lum – oh yeah! Girl I wanna make you sweat...

🕑 *Mon–Fri, 12pm–2.30pm & 6pm–10pm, Sat, 12pm–2.30pm & 6pm–11pm*

💰 *£10.95*

Sukhothai

8 Regent Street, Chapel Allerton

(0113) 237 0141

Dumplings are so hot right now. You will never know the future until you eat at this award winning Thai restaurant just outside of the centre. The staff are so courteous that it makes you sit up and say things like 'Yes please, cola would be fantastic, thanks so much'. There's masses of choice, generous set menus, and the satay will make you rub your tummy with joy. And of course there's the yummy, juicy dumplings. The service is super speedy, so if you want a little breather between courses, be sure to ask when you order.

🕑 *Tue–Sat, 5pm–11pm; Sun, 6pm–11pm*

🍴 *Pad khing, £7.50*

💰 *£10.95*

Eat

The Last Viceroy

145 New Road Side, Horsforth

(0113) 258 0293

It doesn't sound like your typical Indian restaurant and it doesn't really look it, but it does taste like it. One thing is for sure though, and that's whoever you go with you're all sure to find something you like. As befits the last provincial governor of Bengal (aha, see we do research) it ought to be the place to give us the best of its country's cuisine, and the best service that we deserve, and it does. Everything on the menu is worth a tickle, so try their buffet (for pocket change prices), and laugh you way through the whole lot.

🕐 *Mon–Thu, 4pm–12am; Fri–Sat, 4pm–1am; Sun, 12pm–12am*

🍴 *Murgh tikka massala, £6.95*

💳 £11.95

The Slug and Lettuce

14 Park Row

(0113) 244 9209

Well, slap our bare faced cheek and remind us that this is a restaurant because we haven't got a clue what it's trying to be. It's a mixture between something that could be a stylish bar, if it could be arsed, and a brewery pub found on the edge of a dual carriageway gauntlet. Jack of all trades, master of none really. Their nosh is very tasty, affordable, and with a decent choice, but like any chain gastro-joint it gives you that feeling of food déjà vu. Good for a lazy lunch but nothing to shout about.

🕐 *Mon–Thu, 7.30am–10pm; Fri–Sat, 9am–10pm; Sun, 9.30am–10pm*

🍴 *Slug club sandwich, £6.50*

💳 £11.95

The Olive Tree

74–76 Otley Road, Headingley

(0113) 274 8282

Memories of holidays often involve the food, and when you come home to grey Northern skies and even greyer, gritty, flaccid pasties you search relentlessly for a restaurant that can deliver you from the gristly evils of Brit reality and take you back to those hallowed plates of sunshine again. The Olive Tree is such a haven, serving up a happy, friendly, genuine culture along with authentic Greek food to evaporate the rain in your post-trip soul, and prove you don't need to easyJet it for some great Med cooking.

🕐 *Mon–Sat, 12pm–2pm & 6pm–10.30pm; Sun, 12pm–10pm*

🍴 *Lamb kleftiko, £12.50*

💳 £11.95

Trio Bar and Grill

44 North Lane

(0113) 203 6090

Trio has made some odd decisions, like naming the upstairs bar Skippy's, and coating the walls of the downstairs one with what appear to be off-cuts of beige velour tracky bottoms. It's a definite favourite with the Headingley set, so expect a packed bar and a high mullet-to-gullet ratio amongst drinkers; nice selection of beers and cocktails mind, and while the restaurant doesn't give you piles of food on your plate you'll be dreaming about what you had for days afterwards, as well as about the person who served it.

🕐 *Mon–Sat, 5pm–11pm; Sun, 5pm–10.30pm*

🍴 *Moroccan lamb, £13.95*

💳 £10.50

Wagamama

31–32 Park Row

(0113) 243 3468

If you lived on the top floor of a posh city apartment complex (and got the bloody Hoover out more than once every solar eclipse) this would be your interior. Stylish and simple décor, married with friendly staff and long communal tables and benches help create that caring, sharing, yet fast-paced chatty atmosphere this chain is famous for. Grab a bucketload of friends, a bowlful of steamed edamame beans to pop out of their pods straight into your mouth, and prepare to lose half of your meal and gain a taste of everyone else's.

🍴 *Mon–Sat, 12pm–11pm; Sun, 12pm–10pm*

🍴 *Chilli chicken ramen, £7.95*

🍴 *£11.25*

The White House

55 Wetherby Road

(0113) 265 6446

No, not the well-known 1600 Pennsylvania Avenue Washington address littered with scandal and debauchery, this White House is simply your perfect pub. Not to be outdone by the poshest of posh in Leeds, they have a variety of specials that would make Gordon Ramsey whisper sweet nothings into his hearty plate. As for Christmas, lets stop with all the minimalist nonsense and drench ourselves in it like we were kids again. The new management has ensured that in the 2007 elections, we'll be voting for The White House.

🍴 *Mon–Sat, 11am–10pm; Sun, 12pm–9pm*

🍴 *Sausage and mash, £6.65*

🍴 *£9.75*

Wardrobe

6 St Peter Street

(0113) 383 8800

Itchy's second best thing to find in a wardrobe would be Banania: like the C.S. Lewis creation, but replacing endless winter, Turkish delight and cocky toffs called Edmund with eternal summer, many comically-shaped fruits, and thus huge potential for immature nob gags. Best of all, though, would be this excellent restaurant. Fill your tum-nus with the pre-theatre menu before catching a play, or work your way through the mouthwatering specials board before sauntering downstairs for live music.

🍴 *Bar, Mon–Sat, 11am–2am;*
Food, Mon–Fri, 12pm–10pm

🍴 *Honeyed duck with roasted figs, £14*

🍴 *£13*

Zachary's

54 Fulneck, Pudsey

(0113) 256 4069

We've found it: the Holy Grail. Itchy found it. Outside the city, it's a bit of a trek, but worth it. A sweet, family-run place with top notch service that still gives you space to breathe. If they see you're capable of pouring your own wine they won't make you feel like a cripple and top up your glass every thirty seconds. The same kind of food you get in the city but in man-sized portions and with more effort put into the taste and presentation. Get out of the big smoke and spoil yourself for once.

🍴 *Tue–Sat, 6pm–9pm;*
Sun, 10am–3pm & 6pm–9pm

🍴 *Lemon sole, £18.50*

🍴 *£11.20*

Test of moral fibre

ALRIGHT, SO WE'RE ALL SUPPOSED TO BE EATING ETHICALLY NOWADAYS. BUT WHAT WE WANT TO KNOW IS WHETHER ANY OF THE MONKEYS THAT BANG ON ABOUT THIS STUFF HAVE EVER TRIED IT OUT WHEN PICKING UP SOME POST-PUB STOMACH FILLERS. IT'S A BLOODY NIGHTMARE. OBSERVE:

Illustration by Si Clark, www.si-clark.co.uk

1 **Food miles** – According to some environmental fascist or other, it's not ecologically friendly to eat stuff that's been flown across the world when you could chomp on courgettes grown much closer to home. Not according to our friendly burger van, however.

Itchy: 'Excuse me, but how many food miles has that quarter pounder done?'

Burger man: 'What?'

Itchy: 'How many miles has it travelled to end up here?'

Burger man: 'Ten miles, mate. Straight from Lidl to this spot.'

Itchy: 'But what about where it came from originally? What about the sourcing?'

Burger man: 'Saucing? I've got ketchup and mustard, you cheeky sod. And it's free, not like him down the road and his "10p-a-sachet" bollocks, now you gonna buy this burger or what?'

'Reckon you could catch enough fish for all the UK's chippies using a fishing rod?'

2 **Sustainability** – It's not meant to be the done thing to eat fish caught in a way that stops our scaly friends reproducing fast enough to prevent their numbers dropping. Sadly, no-one's told our local chippy.

Itchy: 'Is your cod line-caught?'

Chippy owner: 'Yeah, it's caught mate. How else do you reckon it comes from the sea?'

Itchy: 'No, I'm asking if it was caught using a fishing rod.'

Chippy owner: 'You reckon you could catch enough fish for all the UK's chippies using a fishing rod?'

Itchy: 'Erm, no...'

Chippy owner: 'Right, well there's your answer then.'

Itchy: '...but, you know that you should only really eat fish from sustainable sources don't you?'

Chippy owner: 'Oh yeah? According to who? The media? Reckon all that coke they're on's organic? Produced locally, is it?'

Itchy: 'Well, it's not always possible to consume entirely ethically…'

Chippy owner: 'My point exactly. One cod and chips then is it?'

Drink

Drink

BARS

The Angel's Share
Stainbeck Corner, Harrogate Road, Chapel Allerton
(0113) 307 0111

Religion might have been so very different had the angels stopped off here on their way to spread the holy word; the magi would have received some incomprehensible text message about the 'pon of inf' while the angels got smashed on the verandah. Haul ass here before 1pm on a weekend to swig a Bloody Mary, gobble some breakfast and sip on a huge latte from the giant sofas, all for the bargain price of £6.

ⓒ *Mon–Fri, 11am–12.30am; Sat, 10am–12.30am; Sun, 10am–11pm*
ⓘ *Smoked salmon brunch, £6*
ⓔ *£11.50*

Baby Jupiter
11 York Place
(0113) 242 1202

This retro funk bunker is run by a geezer (or should that be geyser? The guy is one HOT mover) called Smurf, but certainly won't leave you blue. Its allergic-to-house alternative music policy includes fave Itchy night Unkle Munkle Funkle, spinning 60s and 70s cult TV themes and psychedelic lounge classics on the first Thursday of each month, and the whole place oozes groovy cool like its rivals' inferior burgers ooze the fat of losers. Should be re-named Baby Saturn, 'cos it runs rings round the rest.

ⓒ *Mon–Fri, 12pm–11.30pm; Sat, 7pm–11.30pm; Food, Mon–Fri, 12pm–2.30pm*
ⓘ *Chilli cheese burger, £5.50*
ⓔ *£11*

The Arc
19 Ash Road, Headingley
(0113) 275 2223

If you're trying to avoid anyone you've ever known from any era of your life then you must stay away from Arc. On the other hand, if you're up for relighting the fire with an old flame, this is the place you're likely to find them. Very popular, this glass-fronted arc-shaped building is where anyone who lives in Headingley will end up at some point in the night. Relax in the seated areas or dance your wedges off, while keeping yourself tanked up with one of their splendid drinks offers.

ⓒ *Mon–Wed, 11am–12.30am; Thu–Sat, 11am–1am; Sun, 11am–10pm*
ⓘ *Thai chicken burger, £6.95*
ⓔ *£10.50*

Bar Fibre

168 Lower Briggate

(0113) 234 1304

Fibre is like a *Hed Kandi* album cover brought to life: stupidly attractive people in brightly coloured clothes twisting their bones and pouting their bee-stungs. A super-stylish bar with an atmosphere as cool as ice and people that care too much about their appearance, giving it just the right level of pretension to make a hilarious night out. Don't even think about trying to look your best here, there's no way you can compete with the OTT brigade.

🕒 *Mon–Wed, 11am–12am; Thu, 11am–1am; Fri, 11am–6am; Sat, 11am–4am; Sun, 12pm–12am*

🍴 *Lasagne al forno, £6.95*

💲 *£11*

Bar Home

Arch X, Granary Wharf

(0113) 245 6555

If you're ready to risk your pretty little life walking through the shadowy tunnels underneath the station, then put on your hardest expression and leg it on through to Bar Home. You might say it's the proverbial light at the end of the tunnel. Our favourite refuge in the mish mash that is Granary Wharf, you can hide yourself away from the scary, cold, concrete world that lurks outside. Grab yourself some great grub and thank your lucky stars you pulled someone with enough money for a cab to get you safely home.

🕒 *Mon–Wed, 12pm–9.30pm; Thu–Sat, 12pm–11pm; Food, Mon–Sat, 12pm–6pm*

🍴 *Cheesy chips, £1.50*

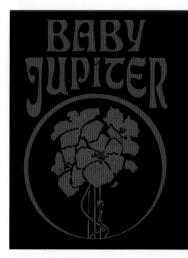

Drink

Boutique

1–15 Hirsts Yard

(0113) 245 6595

Four shots of darkness, six shots of sexy, five shots of style, seven shots of funky music, unlimited shots of high street honey, and money left at the end of the night to sweeten the deal. Throw mixture into perfect sized shaker, add slices of cool and a twist of class, jiggle, and serve with love and a little umbrella to as many of the people of Leeds that know how to appreciate personal service and an atmosphere that is thick with happiness inducing air.

 Mon, 4pm–12am; Tue–Wed, 12pm–12am; Thu–Sat, 12pm–2am; Sun, 12pm–12.30am

 Bacon and black pudding sandwich, £4.95

 Margarita, £6

Chino Latino

Boar Lane, City Square

(0113) 380 4080

Pretend you're sick, wait for your parents to go out, stuff your bed with you-shaped pillows and play a recording of your disease-ridden voice on a loop. Then, pop on your denim, go and TWOC your best friend's dad's Ferrari, pick up the girl of your dreams, see a parade, then drive the Ferrari out of a massive window. Once you've beaten up your headmaster, get over your crazy day off by supping cocktails and grooving in Chino Latino. Ouuum-bop-bop, mmm-chik-chika-chika, ouum-bop-bop, aaaawww chika chika...

 Mon–Sat, 12pm–3am; Food, Mon–Sat 6pm–10.30pm; Sun, 6pm–10pm

 £13.50

The Box

8 Otley Road

(0113) 224 9266

In the middle of what, at night, looks like Yorkshire's answer to Faliraki, The Box is the kind of bar that tends to attract people dressed as overgrown chickens and other such hilarious things. If you're not grown-up enough to know that screeching at the bar staff and waving your money in their faces isn't the way to behave in public, then you'll be fine here. For some reason these sorts of people love it, leaving those of us that aren't squeaky slappers or cocky pricks getting pushed around the bar sober and pissed off.

 Mon–Fri, 10am–11pm; Sat, 10am–1am; Sun, 10am–12.30am

 £6.95–£10.50

Cross Keys

107 Water Lane

(0113) 243 3711

Holbeck. Well, not exactly the Holbeck you're thinking of. This is the part of Leeds that's trying very, very hard to crawl from the depths of scally hell, and it's managing to do so with dignity. If you do happen to wander into this part of town, be careful what you wear to avoid being mistaken for someone who's looking for trade, but be sure to take a trip to the Cross Keys and drink with other hip and stylish people who are happy to sleep with others without asking for money.

 Mon–Sat, 12pm–11pm; Sun, 12.30pm–10.30pm; Food, Mon–Sun, 12pm–4pm & 6pm–10pm

 £11

Dr Wu's

35 Call Lane

(0113) 242 7629

If you've gone out on Call Lane once too often and you're showing symptoms of pretentiousness overload, Dr Wu's can offer you a refreshingly down-to-earth cure. Hidden among some of the trendiest bars in town, this place somehow manages to maintain the feeling of walking into the chill-out room at a mate's house party. There is a definite feeling that people here are more bothered about providing good music than making the room look like a space station, and excellent shows by alternative live bands crank up the atmosphere. Special treatment indeed.

🕒 *Mon–Fri, 5pm–2am; Sat, 2pm–2am; Sun, 5pm–12.30am*

The Elbow Room

64 Call Lane

(0113) 245 7011

Ah finally, a place to go and shoot some pool and pretend we're New York gangstas without worrying about why the dude in the trackie is eyeing up your ciggie. What we love the most is being able to prance around your pool cue like a rock star before launching yourself onto one of the sofas and tucking into your cheesy chips. The Elbow Room plays some of the hippest tunes in town too, so if you know what QOTSA and DFA stand for, we'll see you there, sweet thing.

🕒 *Sun–Thu, 12pm–1am; Fri–Sat, 12pm–2am*

🍴 *Chicken satay, £4.95*

🍸 *Long Island ice tea, £5*

Drink

Fudge

32–34 Assembly Street

(0113) 234 3588

Nails done? Check. Lippy on? Check. Hair tousled and sexy? Check. Accessories on? Check. Posh Spice's look copied? Check. Taxi booked? Oh God, it's here already. Take a deep breath, slow down, no need to rush. Remember, you have the confidence to go out there and turn heads, and you're going to flaunt it in Fudge. Dance, giggle and flirt the night away without the fear that you'll end up waking up realising you slept with a Maggot-from-GLC look-alike. When it's served like it is here, we find that a finger of fudge is just enough to keep Itchy happy.

◎ *Mon–Sat, 8pm–2am*

Jake's Bar

27 Call Lane

(0113) 243 1110

No, no, no, not the dodgy Mr Dean from Hollyoaks, this is someone else's bar, and thank God, 'cos we wouldn't go anywhere near it if it were his. Weirdo. Jake's is full of nooks and crannies (whatever the hell crannies are), so there's plenty of places to hide from that mentalist from work who thinks they're your best mate. But it's not all hidey holes here; there's enough floor space and funky music for the boss to make a complete tit of himself. As for the service, well, bless 'em, it is only a small bar.

◎ *Mon–Thu, 5pm–2am; Fri, 5pm–3am; Sat, 11am–3am*

⊘ *£12.50*

Las Iguanas

Unit 3 Cloth Hall Street

(0113) 243 9533

Las drunkos amongst us are all fully aware of el tequila Mexicana, thu Scoooootash whisky and de Raashan wodka but here's a new one for you: Brazil's national drink, cachaça. A night in Las Iguanas is pretty surreal if you concentrate too hard on the mosaic table tops and Latin fancy wear, but give the native drink a try, it's not as painful as their waxing and not as sharp as their footy team. You never know, you might like it so much you get inspired to rob a train and flee the country for South America.

◎ *Mon–Thu, 12pm–11pm; Fri–Sat, 12pm–11.30pm; Sun, 12pm–10.30pm*

⦿ *Shredded duck enchilada, £8.90*

⊘ *£12.50*

Milo

10–12 Call Lane

(0113) 245 7101

Live gigs, DJ nights, cheap drinks and it's situated on Call Lane. Anything else we need to know, Milo? Sorry who? Kaiser Chiefs? No shit. Well, here's some news for all you pop, rock, and indie kids. It seems that an actual, real life rock star used to work behind the bar here. And from the look of the staff, he's obviously left behind a few style tips, 'cos this place is rocking the look. All of this means that the party kids are loving this venue more and more, so while the Kaiser Chiefs may have sold out, Milo's new code name is 'hot'. Rock on.

🕒 Tue, 5pm–11pm; Wed–Thu, 5pm–1am; Fri, 5pm–2am; Sat, 12pm–2am

The Mixing Tin

9 Albion Street

(0113) 246 8899

Like the *Big Issue* seller who performs in the streets every evening outside Wilko's, The Mixing Tin is not the kind of venue that goes for subtlety when enticing potential customers through its doors. Walking by, head hanging low because you've just spent too much money on stuff you'll probably only wear once, your body is jolted towards the open doors of the basement venue by the loud music blaring out on to the street above. Next time you find yourself fingering that new salmon pink top, put it down, walk away and stop off here for some live music action. That's much more like it, eh?

🕒 Mon–Sat, 12pm 'til late

Décor blimey

Pub décor – boring, eh? Or so you might think. If you're after something with the appeal of a back to back *Button Moon* and munchies session skip over to **Fab Café** (46 Woodhouse Lane, 0113 244 9009). Don't hide behind the sofa when you see Daleks appear – they're just for decoration. Alternative music plays over what looks like the fine ornaments of a geeky teenage boy's bedroom. For something classier, shimmy up to **Normans** (36 Call Lane, 0113 234 3988). Chandeliers, wooden sauna-style walls and the wintry feel of the toilets win it our vote for a cosy night out. If you crave a more retro style, **Baby Jupiter** (11 York Place, 0113 242 1202) has the music, the décor and the atmosphere. Just don't get too comfortable, because you have to go back out into the present day when you leave.

Drink

Mojo

18 Merrion Street
(0113) 244 3687

Rock and indie, old and new. That's what this bar is all about. That, and shed loads of fun. Mojo is a small bar with a massive personality, giving you a global boozing experience, with their range of bottled beers from all over the world. Everyone's welcome here, from students to the young at heart, so it becomes like a big melting pot of guitar band-loving folk of every shape and size. If you're not feeling up for it, splash out on one of their Harlem Mugger cocktails and you'll soon get your Mojo back, baby.

Ⓞ *Mon–Wed, 6pm–11pm; Thu, 6pm–12am; Fri–Sat, 6pm–1am*

❷ *Lime daiquiri, £4.20*

Normans

36 Call Lane
(0113) 234 3988

This place is like having all our childhood fantasies rolled into one – with the exception of that weirdo from IT's warped dreams (see below). Chandeliers, Scandinavian wood and the Narnia toilets all stand together to create a truly delicious bar. It looks totally surreal, but once you get used to it you realize that it's attracting all the right people. There are enough tables to chat around and enough floor space to stand there looking pullable. So anyway, apparently the guy from IT used to imagine that... damn, we're out of space.

Ⓞ *Mon–Tue, 12pm–1am; Wed–Sat, 12pm–2am; Sun, 12pm–12.30am*

❷ *£12*

Mook

Hirst's Yard
(0113) 245 9967

Sounds like an animé movie about a Japanese girl searching for her parents after they were kidnapped by an evil Yakuza gang boss for having superpowers. In reality, it's a superpowered bar, but you do have to wander down an alleyway to find it. The ATM inside allows you to take full advantage of the wondrous drinks offers while the music ranges from high-voltage electro to plugged-in funk, mixed cleanly so you can get messy. Every night. With no door tax. Become a Mooky pup.

Ⓞ *Mon–Sat, 12pm–2am; Sun, 12pm–12.30am; Food, Mon–Sun, 12pm–8pm*

Ⓘ *Club burger, £5.95*

❷ *£8.50*

North Bar

24 New Briggate

(0113) 242 4540

Apart from the fancy artiness of this place, it is essentially a drinker's paradise. If you're seriously pissed off with your boyfriend/girlfriend for fobbing you off for his mates again/nagging at you for fobbing them off for your mates, totter on down to North Bar to forget it all. A warning though: when you wake up the morning after, it may suddenly dawn on you that you drank so much continental beer you're starting to look pregnant. (Perhaps that's why *The Observer* voted it Best Place to Drink in Britain.)

Ⓒ *Mon–Tue, 12pm–1am; Wed–Sat, 12pm–2am; Sun, 12pm–10.30pm*

Ⓐ £11

The Northern Light

Cross York Street

(0113) 243 6446

More tall skinnies than all the Starbucks in a square mile (about 128) put together, Northern Light attracts beauties like moths to a, really attractive, pheromone-soaked lady moth. Who is on fire. Not the place to go if you're feeling slightly inadequate, but rather somewhere to go and strut your funky stuff on one of those near-mythical you're-better-looking-and-taller-than-usual days. If you're willing to suck it up and suck it in, the food here is a real treat and the clubby bar is right back on form as a hot spot to see and be seen after a blip a couple of years back.

Ⓒ *Mon–Sat, 12pm–10.30pm*

Ⓐ £9.50

Drink

Oporto

31–33 Call Lane

(0113) 243 4008

Imagine walking into your perfect living room: leather sofas, exposed red brick and old school beams. Well, your fantasy now has a name: Oporto. With pop, rock and prancy indie, it attracts the boho fashionistas of our slick city, leaving the crowd's Oceana and Creation' to be sick on each other far away. They manage to combine all the essential elements of a good bar to perfection: fuzzy atmosphere, live music, food, honeys and drink. Sound too good to be true? Try chilling here during the day and then get busy with the beer goggles after dark.

🕐 *Mon–Tue, 12pm–12am; Wed–Thu & Sat, 12pm–1am; Fri, 12pm–2am; Sun, 1pm–12am*

Prohibition

Greek Street

(0113) 240 005

Don't be fooled by the name. With over 105 (count 'em) cocktails on their list, there are more than enough tasty routes to drink your way to oblivion in this dark, classy venue. Be prepared to fight your way through a crowd of ex-geek, suited-up businessmen dancing like your dad at a wedding to get to the bar, and then watch while the bartender throws your drink around a bit. Or, you can have your drinks brought directly to your table by one of the very attractive waiting staff and save yourself the hassle.

🕐 *Mon–Wed, 11am–12am; Thu, 11am–1am; Fri–Sat, 11am–2am; Sun, 5pm–2am*

💰 *£11*

Oracle

3 Brewery Place

(0113) 246 9912

Oracle is something special for those who clutter up the city centre with their suits and oversized golfing umbrellas during the day. Someone's done a swanky interior design job, mixing Indian with baroque for maximum luxury effect. Then they've taken half an ounce of naughtiness, a splash of haughtiness, and mixed it with bubbles, a squeak of food porn and funky music in a way that will make you spend all the cash that you worked hard to splash. Lean back, pose and soak it all up.

🕐 *Ground floor, Mon–Sat, 11am–12am; Sun, 10am–10pm; first floor, Mon–Sat, 6pm–2am; Sun, 6pm–12.30am*

💰 *£12.50*

Puro Lounge Bar

50–52 Call Lane

(0113) 243 8666

Puro used to be known as The Fruit Cupboard, and since the takeover they have made every effort to speed up the rotting process and fully clear out the insides. A giant Brillo pad, a ton of bleach and a mountain of style has made Puro into the most promising new start down at The Calls. They're currently a battleground for a serious war between promoters, toughing it out to have their nights held there. One of our current faves is The Breakfast Club; super-funky music and the title of one of the best movies ever made means that we're living the dream 'til 9am on a Sunday morning.

Ⓒ *Times vary*

The Reliance

76–78 North Street

(0113) 295 6060

No, you sillies, not a mispronunciation of a little three wheeled car, but a cool place to rest your boots of an evening. For cosiness and cuddles after a hard day waiting for public transport in the bitter, arctic weather of Leeds, you can rely on this bar and bistro to warm your cockles and loosen that coat belt. Shiver in of an evening for candlelight and Chesterfields, or mooch down on a Sunday to join the ever-increasing hangover ridden population as they refuel and rehydrate their poor, broken, partied-out bodies.

Ⓒ *Mon–Sat, 12pm–11pm;*
Sun, 12pm–10.30pm

Ⓞ *£11.50*

Quid Pro Quo

Greek Street

(0113) 244 8888

So, quid pro quo, eh? Well you won't get us with your fancy lawyers' terms or whatever the hell else it means. Hark at thee with your fancy name for a fancy bar. You'll be asking us whether we have a separate moisturiser for our hands next. Come on, this is Leeds. Helloooo? No need for silly names here you know. All you need to know is that this is a decent place for putting the world to rights over a beer or three. The drinks are cheap enough, the staff are friendly, and a DJ drops in every now and then to keep the toes tapping. 'Nuff said.

Ⓒ *Mon–Thu, 11am–11pm;*
Fri–Sat, 11am–2am

Ⓞ *£7.95*

Drink

Revolution

48 Call Lane
(0113) 243 2778

The daddy of the two Revolutions in Leeds, and situated down the sexiest street in town, this establishment has earned a loyal crowd of customers, with DJs performing every night and house music ruling the roost at weekends. Float around on the dance floor or sit about looking hot. Beware though, as with all Revolution bars, it is near impossible to get a drink without bringing back a tray of brightly-coloured vodka shots to your eagerly awaiting mates; better prepare yourself for a very heavy night.

© *Mon–Sat, 12pm–2am;*
Sun, 1pm–12.30am
❷ *£8*

Sandinista

5 Cross Belgrave Street
(0113) 305 0372

Aww bless, couldn't afford a holiday this year? Or did you just lose your passport, you idiot? Fear not, for as we all know, Leeds does not suffer from rain or snow or cold weather at all. We have the climate of España here, and it seems the bars do too. Or so Sandinista would have us believe. Whether it's The Clash album, or the Nicaraguan political party that inspired the name, it's straight from your holiday memories, so we thank the people who gave it to us from the bottom of our chilly hearts.

© *Sun–Wed, 12pm–1am; Thu, 12pm–2am;*
Fri–Sat, 12pm–3am
⑪ *Spanish ploughman's, £6.95*
❷ *£11*

Revolution Electric Press

41 Cookridge Street, Millennium Square
(0113) 380 4992

You know the score by now – more flavours of vodka on sale than you can squint up and read by the end of the night, shots on sticks and pitchers of cocktails with bits of fruit floating in them. As the second Revolution bar to hit the city centre, this place doesn't really offer Leeds anything 'revolutionary' other than some impressively powerful hand driers in the toilets. It does however seem to be busy most nights, with DJs playing a variety of music from house to urban and alternative. Always a fun and lively atmosphere, especially at weekends.

© *Mon–Sat, 12pm–2am; Sun, 1pm–12.30am*
❷ *£8*

Scene

Park Plaza, City Square

(0113) 380 4000

As close to the train station as is comfortably possible on those nights when the recorded announcer is having a fit and you know that your train is not about to leave the platform any time in the next few years. Nestled in the midst of a lot of very generic-looking bars and restaurants, Scene stands out thanks to its sheer simplicity. A bit of style after a scummy day at work, the bar atmosphere here is is open and fresh. And if your drinking partner suddenly starts getting a bit fresh, then you're not far from a room in the hotel above.

 Mon–Sun, 9am–12am

 £14.95

Townhouse

Assembly Street

(0113) 219 4006

Wants to be Leeds' own Chinawhite, but has more in common with China Black, who had a hit in '94 with *Searching*. We're still searching for a reason to bother with this place. Whatever the people within are hunting for, they often seem to look down their noses for it. Nice cocktails and a stylish location with great potential, but when there are harsh queues to get in, further queues for the loos, and some punters who are too self-important to mind their Ps and Qs... a good night? Get outta town.

 Mon–Wed, 12pm–2am; Thu, 12pm–3am; Fri, 12pm–3.30am; Sat, 12pm–4.30am

 Crayfish and rocket sandwich, £3.50

 £14

Tiger Tiger

The Light, 117 Albion Street

(0113) 236 6999

Although absolutely none of us would if we didn't have to, it's an unfortunate fact of life that we're all forced to go to work or uni on a regular basis, and even though Leeds public transport seems to get worse on gale-force, 'bucket down' days, we can always cover ourselves with a fragile umbrella and run. Thankfully our nights don't need to be at the mercy of the British weather, thanks to the all-round good skills of Tiger Tiger. It's a bar crawl in itself, but with the class you've always found lacking on The Otley Run.

 Mon–Sun, 12pm–2am

 Stir-fried, chilli-drizzled tiger prawns, £9

 £11.95

Trio Bar and Grill

44 North Lane

(0113) 203 6090

Students of Leeds, this is your up market bar. It's yours, we don't want it, you can have it. Well, that's a lie really, because Trio is smart, happy and it plays music for us all. It's only problem is that they manage to squeeze in as many people as possible, and those of us that have even a pinch of decorum in our beautifully toned bodies end up getting thrown around a bit. Pick your spot carefully if you intend to chat and consider everyone else if you fancy a dance, or people will get hurt.

 Mon–Sat, 5pm–12.30am; Sun, 5pm–10.30pm

 Beer battered fish and chips, £10.95

 £12.25

Drink

Wardrobe

6 St Peter Street

(0113) 383 8800

Re-Ward-ing indeed. One of Leeds' best live music venues, especially for stripped-down acoustic and bold-as-brass jazz. Look out for beatboxing events too; pioneer Shlomo has held mindblowing championship heats in their basement club in the past. The bar is lined with those mysterious, perfume-esque, ornate bottles you're always tempted to try; let the skilled staff here guide you through the cocktail list until you're wearing the very best outfit the Wardrobe has to offer – the cosiest beer jacket in the world.

🕒 *Mon–Sat, 11am–2am;*
Food, Mon–Fri, 12pm–10pm
💷 *£13*

PUBS

Adelphi

1–5 Hunslet Road
(0113) 245 6377

No, sadly not the infamous Liverpool hotel with insane staff on hand to pander to your every whim. The Adelphi is a decent pub near enough to ASDA House for them to end up allowing plenty of insurance claims after a liquid lunch, and also close enough to the dear John Smith's brewery to make sure the ale's as tasty as it can be. Just be careful you don't get too comfortable, because you could easily end up with your own tankard there.

🍺 *Sun–Wed, 12pm–11pm;*
Thu–Sat, 12pm–12am
💲 *£9.50*

Barracuda

20 Woodhouse Lane
(0113) 244 1212

The Barracuda: an elongated deep sea swimmer with a very ugly mug. He stalks his pray before pouncing with lightning speed. Known to have taken a cheeky bite out of innocent divers and repented once the taste didn't satisfy his culinary requirements – there you go, we do research our reviews. The bar, however, can be simply described as a place to go after a few too many and providing a good opportunity to dance to *I Don't Like Cricket* in the style of *The Mighty Boosh*.

🍺 *Mon–Wed, 11am–11pm; Thu,*
11am–12am; Fri–Sat, 11am–2am;
Sun, 12pm–11pm
💲 *£9.90*

Bar Censsa

31 Boar Lane
(0113) 244 5220

Depending on how long ago you left school and whether or not you've realised that using your phone as a stereo is a tragic thing to do, you might want to crack a U-turn and head on up to Greek Street for your merriment. Once a crucial stop on your good old pissed-up bar crawl from Squares, this place seems to have fallen into some sort of 'cool hole'. In fact, it's the kind of hole that's very deep, with something slimy and smelly at the bottom. On the other hand, if your daddy's a millionaire, you might like to pop in for a bit of rough.

🍺 *Mon–Wed, 7am–12am; Thu–Sat,*
7am–2am; Sun, 11am–10.30pm
💲 *£8.95*

Drink

Beckett's Bank

28–30 Park Row
(0113) 394 5900

Banks are always such quiet places, aren't they? It's probably because they don't have music playing. Well, that's about the only thing that this pu actually has in common with a bank. Oh, except for the fact that it used to be one. The staff aren't stuffy or smart, the service isn't super formal and they don't take as much money out of your pocket as you seem to pay your bank in overdraft charges every month. That said, it is a Wetherspoons, so beware of the scary vagrants pottering about.

Ⓒ *Mon–Sat, 12pm–11pm;*

Sun, 12pm–10.30pm

Ⓓ *£6.99*

Dry Dock

Woodhouse Lane
(0113) 203 1841

'Ahoy there matey, ye haven't seen me vessel hanging round these parts have ye?' Now we like a pun or two round here, but to be fair, if a man with an eye patch did ask you that question you'd slap a sexual harassment suit on his chops. The Dry Dock is set in the middle of that sea-sick part of town that's invaded by dirty pirate harlots every night, but don't let that put you off. As part of the 'Scream' chain, they offer awesome drinks deals, and if you can get your greedy hands on a yellow card, this place is your first port of call for pure, filthy fun.

Ⓒ *Mon–Sun, 12pm–2am*

Ⓓ *£5.50*

Deer Park

68 Street Lane
(0113) 246 3090

Is it us or does Jimmy Savile tend to get just about everywhere in Leeds? And don't we always want to tell you about it? Now then, now then, why spoil a good run by giving you information to the contrary? So, Itchy is proud to be able reveal to you that Jimmy Savile has been known to take a footstep into this tweedies' fave. It's as civilized as the name would suggest, though the prices of the drinks aren't. So ditch that salmon pink pullover and trot down to the Deer Park, and we're sure they'll fix it for you.

Ⓒ *Mon–Sat, 12pm–11pm;*

Sun, 12pm–10.30pm

Ⓓ *£8.50*

The Eldon

190 Woodhouse Lane
(0113) 245 3591

Jointly named after everyone's most hated comedian and the 'Queen' of pop, this pub is simply one of your standard common or garden boozers. Giving students a good reason to skip lectures and learn about food, lager and football, it is perfectly situated to offer up some real life education. The introduction to this alternative degree takes place on the Otley Run, so make sure you've done your homework and know where to come. We just can't figure out why they named it after Ben Eldon and Eldon John.

Ⓒ *Mon–Wed, 11.30am–11pm; Thu–Sat, 11.30am–12am; Sun, 12pm–10.30pm*

Ⓓ *£7.45*

The Faversham

1–5 Springfield Mount

(0113) 243 1481

Tucked away on Leeds Uni campus, this is a nerve centre of the city's social scene cunningly disguised as a pub. Owned by the people behind HiFi and Wire, succulent music is served in phat portions, along with gourmet burgers, plenty for veggie tables, and a Sunday roast meaner than a selfish fat kid with a bag of sherbet pips and a knuckle duster. They have a different food or drink offer every day, and you can even pre-order grub over the blower. A stunning Yorkshire pudding of a venue, overflowing with the very Bisto best of all things gravy.

🍷 *Mon–Thu, 12pm–2am; Fri, 12pm–3am; Sat, 9am–3am; Sun, 12pm–12.30am; Food, Mon–Sun, 12pm–7pm*

The Grove

Back Row

(0113) 243 9254

After many a good year up in the mean streets of Byker, Ant and Dec thought they'd cash in on their massive success and open a youthie of their own in Leeds. This is a cosy bastion of independent sanity in an area of town that's rapidly turning into a chain gang nightmare. Thank God that they refuse to allow any pretentiousness to cross their threshold, because it's places like this that keep us from losing all faith. Get some real ale down you and listen in to the live acoustic music played every night. If you don't like that kind of thing, you could always go paintballing.

🍷 *Mon–Sat, 12pm–11pm; Sun, 12pm–10.30pm*

Fenton

161 Woodhouse Lane

(0113) 245 3908

About as diverse as a BBC equal opportunities policy and as quintessentially British pub-like as The Rovers Return. If you're a rebellious student wishing to while away your days avoiding the faculty, head elsewhere. However, if you're a rebellious student wishing to while away your days getting afternoon drunk and chatting up members of the faculty then this is definitely the place to guzzle. You never know who you might find here, so you may get lucky and discover that underneath the slumbering forms of the passed-out lecturers lie a couple of stray exam papers.

🍷 *Mon–Fri, 11.30am–11pm; Sat, 12pm–11pm; Sun, 12pm–10.30pm*

Drink

Headingley Taps

32 North Lane
(0113) 220 0931

Out of place for two reasons. The first reason is that, despite being located in what looks like the setting for the new *Futurama* series, it's older than a Des O' Connor gag. The second's that when you go in you realise it's not the mansion-size building that it looks like from the outside, but is both the same size as, and decorated like a council flat specifically designed for Ronnie Corbett. However, we are not snobs, so we refuse to stay away from the beer garden and drinks deals that it has to offer. What open-minded people we are.

🕑 *Sun–Thu, 11am–12am;*
Fri–Sat, 12pm–2am
🍸 *£4.99*

Hyde Park Social Club

Ash Grove
(0113) 293 0109

Unless you're a hippy, you probably won't be too impressed by the interior of the Hyde Park Social. The place looks like a sixth form common room and its 'anything goes' attitude means the regulars treat it like one, too. Upon stepping in, you might wonder why the place smells of wet dog, but once you're greeted by the 90 year old blind mutt and its very friendly owner, you'll soon get it. You'll feel so at home it's easy to forget that you're supposed to pay for drinks. That said, you couldn't make much of a dent in your bank balance here if you tried.

🕑 *Mon–Sat, 2pm–11pm; Sun, 2pm–10.30pm*
🍸 *Double spirit and mixer, £1.50*

The Library

229 Woodhouse Lane
(0113) 244 0794

Oh, how clever those 'Scream' people are. Where do students go when they say they are off to the library? The pub. But The Library is the pub. No, we mean the pub is The Library. No... we mean the books are drinks. Or no... the drinks are books... what? Words are bubbles, thoughts are hops, library cards are yellow, oh man that's it, the trees do go round the sun, yeah they do. No, you're wrong, right? So they navigate what... Hmm, maybe we've spent too much time in The Library, and not enough in the library.

🕑 *Mon–Wed, 12pm–1am; Thu–Sat,*
12pm–2am; Sun, 12pm–12.30am
🍸 *£5.95*

The New Inn

68 Otley Road

(0113) 224 9131

As one of the early stops on the infamous Otley Run itinerary, this is not the place to come to escape gangs of drunkards, or unfortunately, the rather overpriced drinks of central Headingley. From midday onwards, during term time, you can expect to see a variety of oddly-dressed, raucous gangs of youths downing shots at the bar. However, should you tire of watching Superman and the 118 dude battling it out at a game of pool, the New Inn does provide pleasant front and back outdoor seating areas to get away from it all.

🕒 *Mon–Sat, 11am–11pm;*

Sun, 12pm–10.30pm

💷 *£8.95*

Original Oak

2 Otley Road

(0113) 275 1322

There's nothing finer than the buzz of inebriated summer mischief in the packed garden of this West Yorkshire institution. You haven't 'done' Leeds until you've been to The Oak when the barbie's sizzling, the sun's setting over the horizon and LS6's ne'er-do-wells have come out to play. None of your fancy £4 cocktails or beardy real ales here, just a diverse congregation who gather to practice the great British pastime of getting smashed. Locals rub shoulders with sports fans topping up the booze levels after a day at the nearby cricket and rugby grounds. A classic.

🕒 *Mon–Sat, 11am–11pm; Sun, 12pm–10.30pm*

💷 *£4.99*

Drink

The Packhorse

208 Woodhouse Lane

(0113) 245 3980

As you might be able to guess from the fact that it's named after a mode of transportation that went out with anaesthetic-free surgery, this pub ain't no spring chicken. The décor isn't much to write home about (unless of course your family have a thing for tired pub interiors), but the collection of local music lovers that head here don't seem too bothered. If you're after catching a bit of local live talent before they hit the big time, then this is the place to do it. But don't be expecting a classy night out.

🕒 Mon–Sat, 12pm–11pm;

Sun, 12pm–10.30pm

💰 £7.50

The Royal Park

39 Queens Road

(0113) 275 7494

No, you're not going to find Prince Harry hiding in a bush, secretly toking on a crafty bifter here, but with a basement that doubles up as a cosy little gig and open mic venue, you might well find one of the exclusive secret shows this place occasionally puts on. The upstairs has the kind of dog-eared charm that'd associate the place more with the *Royle Family* than the Royal Family, or at least it would if it weren't for all the students milling round in here, killing time on the pool tables between lectures. Still, at least that mean's there's always some to challenge to a game if you're feeling competitive.

🕒 Mon–Sat, 12pm–11pm; Sun, 12pm–10.30pm

Roundhay Fox

Princes Avenue

(0113) 246 3090

We defy you to visit this cosy, traditional pub and not spend the following few days trying to come up with excuses to head there again and again. In summer it's a perfect place to wake yourself up after a sunbathe (or numb the pain of the sunburn) with a refreshing beer, and come the sabbath they do a mean Sunday lunch. Now if only the price of a glass of wine wasn't steeper than the downwards trajectory of Michael Barrymore's career path, we wouldn't be able to stop ourselves raving about this Foxy little venue.

🕒 Mon–Sat, 11am–11pm;

Sun, 12pm–10.30pm

💰 £8.95

The Skyrack

2 Otley Road

(0113) 278 1519

Despite being set in the part of town that's usually synonymous with trendy bars and clubs, the Skyrack's the kind of friendly local boozer you'd expect to find at the end of your road. Once you're inside, it's mercifully unpretentious – the old-fashioned décor makes a refreshing change from the rest of the area's poncey nonsense, and the eerily friendly door staff enjoy a joke with punters, so no worries about being super sensible as you approach. Head here on a weeknight when you don't fancy being hassled by the wasters.

Mon–Tue, 11am–11pm; Wed–Sat, 11am–12.30am; Sun, 12pm–12.30am

£6.80

Stick or Twist

Merrion Way

(0113) 234 9748

There's not much you can say about a Wetherspoons that's not full of pub clichés and generic statements. But then considering that the chain itself is made up of a collection of generic pub clichés, it's hardly surprising. The alcohol's a reasonable price, the lights stay pretty bright and the music's as non-existent as Jordan's singing talent. The décor's a modern/tacky take on the old boozer style, incorporating a casino theme. Which makes a change, considering that the people that run this chain usually react to experimentation worse than those 'elephant man' drug trial peeps.

Sun–Thu, 9am–12am; Fri–Sat, 9am–1am

£6.99

Drink

Strawberry Fields

159 Woodhouse Lane

(0113) 243 1515

With Strawberry Fields' great choice of vegan and vegetarian dishes, they were hardly going to call it Cow Fields or Sheep Fields. Providing you can fight your way through the crowds of ravenous students refuelling on ridiculously cheap pizza and absinthe, you're onto a big, drunken winner. If you're keen on drinking somewhere that doesn't look like it was put together by *Scrapheap Challenge* contestants on acid, we'd suggest giving it a miss. Maybe we're just being fussy, but this is definitely not first date material. Maybe second if you're lucky enough. And skint.

🍸 *Mon–Thu, 6.30pm–11pm;*
Fri–Sat, 6pm–11pm

The Swan

Swan Street

(0113) 244 9130

If you're trying to give a bar a new identity and are stuck for names, look no further than the trustworthy road sign. Pacific is now The Swan, on Swan Street, in Swanville, United Swanses. Aside from the pub-like, slightly unimaginative name, they have assaulted the weekend by accommodating DJs and taken a little bit of time over the once tired-looking décor. Use and abuse before skipping through to the City Varieties and savour the hot summers (they get them in the United Swanses you know) with an afternoon skive.

🍸 *Mon–Wed, 11am–11pm; Thu–Sat,*
11am–1am; Sun, 11am–10.30pm

💷 £7

The Victoria Inn

28 Great George Street

(0113) 246 1386

So, what do we need from a pub? Let's be honest, all we really need is a steady supply of booze, a bar to prop us up straight, somewhere to sit and mumble, and preferably a toilet (unless the landlord doesn't mind you watering his shrubs). Therefore, the Victoria Inn has everything. But no more. There's a definite 'no frills' policy going on here, with no big screen TV, no DJ, and none of the other crowd-pulling shenanigans you might expect of pubs nowadays. In here, they rely on conversation and alcohol for their entertainment. Yeah, we know. Whatever next, eh?

Mon–Sat, 11.30am–11pm

Walkabout

67–83 Cookridge Street

(0113) 205 6500

Go during the day and the red floor makes you think you missed a stonker of a bloodbath the night before. Go at night and if you've any sense you'll be too hammered to notice the floor, or the atrocious entertainment. This isn't a place you go to get drunk, you go here because you ARE drunk. Choose your night carefully or what you expected to be a rip curl of an evening out could better resemble sitting in a retirement home watching the cricket with your granddad (if, of course, your granddad has a habit of wearing short leather skirts and full slap makeup).

Mon, 11am–11pm; Tue, 11am–12am; Thu, 11am–1am; Wed & Fri–Sat 11am–2am

£5.95

Games for a laugh

Finding a pool table may be easy, but what about some games that are a little bit different? **Sela** (20 New Briggate) has no daylight, so it's fully candlelit to get you in the mood. There are a variety of board games on offer from battle ships to chess. Or if you're looking for somewhere more upbeat, the **Dry Dock** (Woodhouse Lane) is always a reliable favourite. You'll only miss it if you think a massive boat at the top of Leeds is normal. Board games are readily available though used bafflingly little. And good news peeps, games night is back at **The Packhorse** (208 Woodhouse Lane), join in or BYO. If none of that takes your fancy then you can always play spot the slapper in **Oceana** (16–18 Woodhouse Lane).

Drink

Whitelocks

Turks Head Yard
(0113) 245 3950

Whitelocks is Leeds' oldest pub, hidden in the depths of one of the city's more obscure alleyways. Bizarrely, despite tourists and legless students alike struggling to find it, the pissed OAPs seem to locate their place at the bar every time. Crinklies aside, this has been described by many as one of, if not THE best city pubs. Great for real ale and real food. Depending on your taste for real ale, finding it may actually be easier than leaving it: take the easy route and hijack a super speedy granny mobile, or pray for a (White)lock-in.

◉ *Mon–Sat, 11am–11pm;*
Sun, 12pm–10.30pm
◔ *£9.95*

Woodies Ale House

104 Otley Road
(0113) 278 4393

Not only is Woodies the first stop on the Otley Run, but it's also the pub that *Fat Friends* was filmed in. And thus we come to the end of The Woodies' achievements. It's quiet, it has a pool table, it serves beer, and it's a pub. That's it. If you've been on the Otley Run, are a major fan of *Fat Friends* (or if you are a character in *Fat Friends*) then you've probably been here, otherwise you probably haven't. Not that this is any great loss, because even if you had you probably wouldn't remember it. And we don't mean 'cos you'd have got so pissed, either.

◉ *Mon–Sat, 11am–11pm;*
Sun, 12pm–10.30pm
◔ *£7.95*

Stay regular

Illustration by Joly Braime

AIN'T NOTHIN' QUITE LIKE STEPPING INTO A BAR AND BEING GREETED AS ONE OF THEIR OWN. HERE'S ITCHY'S GUIDE TO BECOMING AS REGULAR AS CLOCKWORK SOMEWHERE NEW

1 Learn the name of the publican's partner/pet/mum – Take a couple of mates and stand at the bar within earshot of the publican and engage in the 'what would your porn name be?' game (combine your pet's name with your mum's maiden name). After a while, get the publican to join in, and make up some new variants designed to extract info about the names of spouses, dad, etc. Next time you walk in, you'll be able to greet them with a friendly, 'Alright Dave, how's Sandra doing?'

2 Have your own pint mug – Take a vessel and ask them to keep it behind the bar for you. Then whenever you walk in, you can sup your beverage in style. You may want to save this for the second visit.

3 Know the pool rules – If they've already got a set of rules in place, learn what they are, loiter near the table and make sure you pounce upon any infraction to loudly proclaim 'That's not how we do things in here'. If there are no house rules, even better – make some up, don't tell anyone what they are, and then soon everyone'll need to ask you before playing.

4 Start a cribbage team – Unless the pub in question's populated by incontinent octogenarians, there's no chance that they'll have one. Get a 'Captain' T-shirt, and swan round asking randoms if they're ready for the big match. They'll have no idea what you're talking about, allowing you to explain your importance to the pub community.

5 Take a dog – Everyone loves a dog. Well, except asthmatics. But who cares about them? Those guys are already having enough of a wheeze.

IF YOU'RE AFTER GUILTY PLEASURES, WHY NOT GO FOR THE OLD CLASSICS? NO, NOT PROSTITUTION AND PICKING YOUR SCABS, BUT CHEESE AND KITSCH

We all have our guilty pleasures. Luckily, Leeds has plenty of shamefully blissful places. **Fab Café** (46 Woodhouse Lane, 0113 244 9009) is the ultimate in retro kitsch. It's an eccentric bar that pays homage to all things of the past, with memorabilia ranging from Dangermouse to the Daleks. Fab has an array of music, some of it tasteful, some of it naff, but for a bit of nostalgic fun, it can't be beaten. As for cheesy clubs, none can beat the true tackiness of **Baja Beach Club** (43a Woodhouse Lane, 0113 245 4088). The décor includes pictures of surfers, a massive hanging shark protruding from the ceiling, and bikini-clad dancers roaming the floor. The clientele is mostly students looking for a bit of poptastic fun and cheap and cheerful jelly vodka shots (which are sold by the bucket-load). Go to Baja to indulge in the kind of fun we all hate to admit that deep down we really love.

Guilty pleasures

Illustration by Si Clark
www.si-clark.co.uk

Dance

Dance

CLUBS

Baja Beach Club

43a Woodhouse Lane
(0113) 245 4088

We all grew up on *Neighbours* and *Home and Away* and still feel the need to surround ourselves with beach type memorabilia and scantily clad hotties. Although you won't find The Hoff behind the bar (unfortunately), the staff dutifully attire themselves in bikinis or shorts. Cheese is the key, and as a result you'll find more students here than at a Hare Krishna curry stand. Still, it's always a bonus when you get the chance to touch up the staff when they go off on one of their dancing fits, or get cosy in the Jacuzzi.

🕒 *Tue–Thu, 10pm–2.30am;*
Fri–Sat, 10pm–3am

The Blank Canvas

Granary Wharf,
Dark Neville Street
(0113) 244 6570

If you like walking another path, get off track by heading under the train station and brush up on your knowledge of what a really intense club night is all about. Once a month things liven up here with Federation, and get really kicking with live bands like The Music and Cooper Temple Clause. Taking up 12 of Granary Wharf's atmospheric orifices, it's a special place that seems to mould to fit whatever crowd are going wild in the darkness on any given night. You are the paint, it is the canvas. See you on the flip side.

🕒 *First Sat of the month, 10pm–4am*
💷 *£10–£15*

Bar Risa

Units 1–4 The Cube, Albion Street
(0113) 247 1759

There are two major benefits to this venue. One is that it is attached to Jongleurs, so you don't need to go far for a night out after the comedy, and two is that if you can't be arsed to queue for anywhere decent or you've been turned away for wearing trainers, you'll get in because they either have a relaxed dress policy or they are too busy ogling the ladies to notice. Bounce around to hip hop and r 'n' b, take the piss out of the stiff looking posers while the chavs take the piss out of you, and get wasted as you dance like you've never danced before.

🕒 *Sun–Wed, 12pm–2am;*
Thu–Sat, 12pm–3am

Boutique

11–13 Hirsts Yard
(0113) 245 6595

Sweaty guys, drinking pints, coming on to you with the most useless chat-up line you ever heard. Scary looking girls, dripping in gold, eyeing you up if you show any attempt at politeness as they barge into you. No more, we say. No more. We're sick of being shoved into on the dance floor when we're trying to shimmy and look cool, so we're moving on. Those days are over, and we don't miss them one little bit. How have we done it? By coming here of course. Boutique is the way forward and the only place to avoid all of the above.

🕒 *Mon–Sat, 4pm–2am;*
Sun, 4pm–12.30am
💷 *Prices vary*

BRB (Bar Room Bar)

37 Call Lane

(0113) 243 0315

Ok, so it may be part of an evil, bloodsucking chain, and there may be squillions of them up and down the land, but this particular one ain't your average bar. Located at the cooler end of town, serving quality fodder with regular 2-4-1 offers and happy hour deals, the real beauty of this place becomes clear when the weekend begins. As the bar fills, some of the finest local disc-spinning talent frequents the decks, the party people get their groove on and keep going 'til long into the night. Not bad for a bar in a room with a bar.

Sun–Thu, 12pm–12am; Fri–Sat, 12pm–2am; Food, Mon–Sun, 12pm–10pm; Happy hour, daily, 5pm–7pm

Club Mission

8–13 Heaton's Court

(08701) 220 114

Hip-swingers, this is your mission if you choose to accept it: rendezvous at a pumping bar full of other funky cats like you. Sample an array of alcoholic drinks to test for deadly poison then, once you get the all clear, move on to your next checkpoint – the club. Once inside, slip out of your thermal clothing and detonate your lethal booty wiggle. The final part of your mission is to penetrate the dance floor and get in touch with the music. Remember, looks can kill, and you're fully licensed. If you succeed, we all stay cool; if you fail, you will be exiled to Creation. Do your duty, and good luck.

Times vary

Dance

The Cockpit

Swingate

(0113) 244 1573

The Cockpit is the kind of filthy guitar den that its name seems to suggest. Spend more than 15 seconds here and we promise you'll bump into some skinny guy with big, naturally curly hair who could be any one of Wolfmother, or some girl with long, straight dark hair or massive white hair and black eyes. Songs by The Kills, The Rapture, The Music and all of the other 'The' bands will all be heard at a night out here. Go to the vintage shop, eat at an expensive restaurant, then shimmy on down in your pointy shoes and tight jackets for an indie prance. We love it like we love cold lager.

🎧 *Times vary*

Discotheque

54 New Briggate

(08704) 282 726

Firmly taking over where the 'Crasher kids' of Sheffield left off all those years ago, Discotheque is the cool and stylish little sister of the world-famous Gatecrasher. It's a move forward from pure trance, making use of funky up-beats and twisted samples as the way to get bodies pulsing on the dancefloor. The wasted, person-unfriendly décor adds to its attraction for a more upmarket clientele, although that goes the other way too, and what you will definitely see here are those that take way too much time over their tacky, celeb-copying looks.

🎧 *Times and prices vary according to event*

Dirty Disco @ Northern Light

Cross York Street

(0113) 243 6446

Dirty Disco by name, not so disco by nature. In fact, so far from disco you'd probably pop your techno clogs trying to bridge the gap. With international DJs and local heroes pumping out premium rate techno, electro and really filthy house, this is the ultimate way to start your month off in style. It attracts an eclectic mix of the cool, the uncool, the don't-give-a-damn and the downright random, though by the end of the night, no-one gives a shit about anything except getting to the after-party downstairs; aptly named Very Very Wrong Indeed. Seriously.

🎧 *First Sat of every month, 10pm–6am; Very Very Wrong Indeed, 6am–Lunch*

🎧 *Dirty Disco, £10–£15; VVWI, £6*

Evolution

Cardigan Fields Leisure Complex,
Kirkstall Road

(0113) 263 2632

'Hmm, let's think about it – a cinema, a gym, restaurants – what else can we stick in our little entertainment village? Oh, I know, let's put a nightclub in there too. No. Are you kidding? It'll be great. There's young 'uns everywhere here. We can make it like the nightclubs everyone used to go to when they were sixteen and we can have surf machines, rodeos, cheap drinks and general cheese. Oh they'll love it.' Well, we don't actually. It's awful. If you don't agree with us, then put this book down very slowly, put your hands in your pockets, and keep walking 'til the top of your head gets wet.

◑ *Mon–Tue & Thu–Sat, 10pm–2.30am*

The HiFi Club

2 Central Road

(0113) 242 7353

www.thehificlub.co.uk

High five to HiFi for putting Leeds on the map with a golden, star-shaped pin. Its basement placement may make it small, yet this midget gem couldn't be more on the cutting edge of music if it were sliced and diced. Legend of legends is the Move On Up night, approaching a decade of playing northern soul, Motown and funk, but don't miss Harlem Bush Club for live jazz, Saturday comedy, tuneage and roastage at the Sunday Joint and smiley post-work gigs at Teatime Shuffle. Say hi to HiFi, your new bestest friend.

◑ *Times vary*

❷ *Free–£5*

The Faversham

1–5 Springfield Mount

(0113) 243 1481

Host more starry nights than NASA, and everything they launch takes off. Tunes range from indie, electro and rock at Saturdays' Bad Sneakers to funk, breaks, reggae and hip hop at Fridays' New Bohemia – which, with its record and tuck shop, wins new awards every nanosecond. The Fav crew draw big names, but also have a knack at spotting new talent that's going places, and making sure that this is the first place they go. Try acoustic/nu-folk on Sundays for an alternative chill; you mightn't imagine it's your kinda cuppa, but there's good things brewing, we promise.

◑ *Mon–Thu, 12pm–2am; Fri, 12pm–3am;*
Sat, 9pm–3am; Sun, 12pm–12.30am

Dance

High Fibre Breakfast @ Bar Fibre

168 Lower Briggate

(08701) 200 888

Breakfast. Deemed by many to be the most important meal of the day, yet it comes in so many varieties. Full English, continental, champagne, cold pizza. The list is endless... But the good people at Bar Fibre have rustled up their own addition that'll keep your movements regular while being good enough to keep you coming back for more. The ingredients are simple: take one late licence, a bar full of party people, two DJs and oodles of electro, dirty and funky house. Mix vigorously for four hours then serve with a generous side order of shake-your-booty.

🕐 *Fri, 2am–6am*

💷 *£4*

My House

1 Brick Street

(0113) 247 0606

As with your house, our house, and in fact as with just about any house, My House is a place where you can party through the night the way it's meant to be done and then chill until sunrise when you can't take the mayhem any more. Stinky's Peephouse, as it's still affectionately known, is the place to track down the world-renowned hard dance mash-up that is BacktoBasics. And it doesn't need to end there. Make the most of your weekend by sauntering over to Back2mine on Sunday if you're looking for a quick way to get the sack on Monday morning.

🕐 *Fri, 10pm–6am; Sat, 10pm–8am;*
Sun, 9am–10pm

Puro Lounge Bar

50–52 Call Lane

(0113) 243 8666

See what they've done? They've taken all of the 'Fruit' in the 'Cupboard' and mushed it up until it's an unrecognisable purée: Puro. Good lord, how witty of them. It really is quite delightfully clever. Ok, so it's a bit rubbish, but they have done Call Lane a favour by continuing its trend of hosting the most exclusive and stylish bars in town. Puro is a funky house and soul kind of venue with promoters fighting to hold their nights there. So we shouldn't take the piss out of the name, because everything else is the perfect blend of cocktails, smooth music and inspiring décor. Puro brilliance.

🕐 *Times vary*

Quilted Llama & Halo

Trinity St David's Church, Woodhouse Lane

(0113) 245 9263

'Our father, who art in heaven, hallowed be thy name, thy kingdom come, thy will be done, on earth as it is in Halo. Drinketh the most righteous spirits in the land, moveth to the most well known cheese in the universe and when your work is done, falleth into the deepest gutter in the street. Amen.' We're guessing that when the church was built for the good people of ye olde worlde Leeds, they had no idea that the future would come up behind it and kick it in the arse by allowing a uni to be built around it and thousands of students to flock there for some of the devil's own kind of fun.

Ⓒ *Mon–Sun, 9pm–3.30am*

Rehab

2 Waterloo House, Assembly Street

(0113) 244 9474

Rehab has been given a good dose of its own medicine as SpeedQueen saves its life. Not that we weren't up for a bit of Rehab in the first place, but let's be honest, this town is a-growing, and now there are more nightspots than ever, the competition's getting fierce. Especially when the nights move to a better venue. Nevertheless, a bit of hip hop, a load of funky house and wall-to-wall honeys and homeys bumpin' and grindin' make Rehab a whole lot sweeter. Let's hope its recovery keeps going from strength to strength.

Ⓒ *Mon–Wed, 9.30pm–2.30am; Thu, 10pm–3am; Fri, 10pm–4am; Sat, 10pm–6am; Sun (once a month), 10pm–4am*

The Subculture

66 Merrion Street

(0113) 245 0689

An alternative venue this one, offering different nights for different tastes. It's especially popular with black-leather-and-lace-loving fans of bands whose names sound like horror films. If you're tired of being looked at funny and your perfect day is spent in Forbidden Planet hugging your friends, then mooch into Subculture and swing your coloured dreadlocks about in the company of like-minded souls. And even if you don't look like a highwayman who's rubbed flour on his face, everybody here will be very welcoming and will love the fact that you're really into the music.

Ⓒ *Times vary*

Dance

The West Indian Centre

10 Laycock Place

(0113) 262 9496

The closest you'll get to a proper rave without Marty McFly-ing back to a field in 1992. Hard techno, psy trance and dubby chill spills out of two neon rooms onto the grass outside. Hippie poi-fairies and fluoro-souled cyber puppies alike gather until silly o'clock for massive nights like Riff Raff and Cabbage – presumably so-called as you feel like a vegetable for days after. But a very happy vegetable. Perhaps some fluffy mashed potato, with a little pool of melting butter where your troubles used to be, and possibly another where your brain once dwelled. A real experience to remember, if you're able.

☻ *Late, until the sun is high in the sky*

Wire

2–8 Call Lane

(0113) 234 0980

Down to the Wire then for Itchy, to join the sweaty, red indie-uns a-whoopin' and a-hollerin' in delight at all their favourite alternative rock tunes being pumped out by the geniuses who gave them HiFi and the Fav. And you thought being happy in the presence of a Morrissey track was impossible, if not illegal. Presumably named after the width of the vacuum-packed skinny jeans that are the uniform of its backcombed and beamingly bouffant crowd, Wire couldn't be much more of a hit if gave out Noel Fielding-shaped lollipops on the door. As usual, this lot have a great night well and truly licked.

☻ *Times vary according to event*

HEN PARTIES

Distinguishing features: Normally perform their all-female pre-mating ritual in a circular dance around sequined receptacles containing grooming apparel. The leader usually wears a letter L and some kind of sexual apparatus on her head.

Survival: For males under 60, camouflage is the best bet. Itchy recommends a bright pink mini-skirt, padded boob tube and red lippy.

HOMO NARCOTICUS

Distinguishing features: This unusual subspecies is mesmerised by repetitive rhythms and flashing lights, and has a peculiar ability to move all limbs and appendages at once in contrary directions, including eyes and ears.

Survival: These malcos are guaranteed to spill your drink on themselves. Put your bev in a bike bottle or go the whole way and throw a sacrificial pint at them before you start dancing.

Safe and sound

Illustration by Thomas Denbigh

THE DANCE-FLOOR IS A SCARY REALM. IF YOU WANT TO MAKE IT OUT ALIVE, YOU'LL NEED SOME INSIDER KNOWLEDGE, SO GRAB PITH HELMET AND GLO-STICKS AND FOLLOW ITCHY ON A DISCO SAFARI

THE LADS

Distinguishing features: Alpha males indulging in competitive play, such as mixing several beverages in the same glass, and then drinking the whole lot as quickly as possible.

Survival: A propensity to punch the air during power ballads can lead to injury among taller adventurers. Itchy suggests you don a helmet and hit the deck if you hear the line 'Oooh baby do you know what that's worth?'.

UNDERAGE DRINKERS

Distinguishing features: Identified by greasy hair, pale skin and vacant eyes, this genus often regurgitate upon themselves, presenting a hazard to bystanders. Females are impervious to cold and wear very little.

Survival: Enlist their natural predators – larger and more primitive hominids called bouncers, who covet the hair of the underage drinkers, being themselves a furless species.

Gazing at the stars

THERE'S NOTHING LIKE A GOOD CELEB SPOT TO MAKE YOUR DAY SEEM MORE EXCITING TO FRIENDS. HERE'S A RUNDOWN OF WHO YOU'RE LIKELY TO SEE IN LEEDS

So, we all know that Leeds is as cool as an ice cube in Iceland but when you've got some of the sweetest music erupting from it, are you surprised? **Kaiser Chiefs** are the most well-known band to rock out of Leeds in recent years but Itchy has a special place in our heart for alternative rock band **The Music**.

The Wedding Present came from Leeds, and they share a world record with Elvis. Top among the angels, sweet soul singer, the Leeds-born **Corinne Bailey Rae** can be seen pottering about town when she's not being a high-flying singer elsewhere, and as if you couldn't tell by his accent, **Leigh 'Avid Merrion' Francis** is also a fellow Loiner. Take a wild guess where the man with the neck brace got his name from…

Back to music, and apologies to Wakefield, but we're afraid that we're going to have to steal **The Cribs** and pretend they're from Leeds. We love them and they seem to love us. Oh well.

And that's before we've mentioned **Scary Spice**, **Chris Moyles**, **Chumbawumba**, **Vic Reeves** and, our very own favourite author, **Barbara Taylor Bradford**.

Gay

Gay

BARS

Blayde's

Blayde's Yard, Lower Briggate

(0113) 244 5590

If you've long since left uni, Blayde's will bring back all of the memories of going on a big night out, and if you're still at uni this is the place where those memories will come from. It's not a huge bar, but it's partly cramming all those people into such a small space that makes Blayde's as mad as it is. The bar staff are all into pretending they are abroad, performing dance routines at random throughout the evening, which makes for one hell of an atmosphere.

🕒 *Mon–Thu, 2pm–11pm; Fri–Sat, 2pm–1am; Sun, 2pm–12.30am*

💷 *£2.80 per glass*

The New Penny

52 Call Lane

(0113) 243 8055

It's official (well, almost) – Leeds is one of the easiest-going cities around, and the gay scene in this sexy city is one of ever-expanding horizons. The New Penny is another comfortable bar for girls and boys that just wanna have fun. Dress up pretty and get together for a wild night out playing the floor here – there's no doubt that you'll end up doubling your entourage before hitting the town's dizziest heights of queer-dom. And if you ever feel like you're not the brightest penny, a visit here will certainly buff you up.

🕒 *Mon–Tue, 10am–11pm; Wed–Sat, 12pm–2am; Sun, 2pm–12.30am*

💷 *£9*

The Bridge Inn

1–5 Bridge End

(0113) 244 4734

This is the Pleasantville of gay venues in Leeds. All ages mixing it up like a mince pie at Christmas without anyone batting a beautifully decorated eyelid. Watch out for karaoke night on a Thursday because you're more than likely to run in to the next star of the *X Factor* out-takes. Even if you don't meet a true musical horror it's still more than worth a visit for the comedy and giggles. If you're a puppy in the market this is a super friendly crowd, so just remember the old adage: a stranger is a friend you haven't met yet.

🕒 *Mon–Wed, 12pm–12am; Thu–Sat, 12pm–2am; Sun, 12pm–12.30am*

💷 *Becks, £1.50 a pint, 2pm–7pm*

Queens Court

167 Lower Briggate

(0113) 245 9449

'M'lud, the defendant is accused of reckless self-enjoyment with intent to inflict exhaustion and euphoria on their own person.' 'And how does the defendant plead?' Guilty, your honour. Guilty as sin. Itchy's been going down Queens Court for years, and it just goes to show that the original is always the best. Sprawling over two floors, with bars, dancefloors and an outside courtyard for the summer months, we just had to dance. And if that's a crime, then cuff us up officer.

Ⓒ *Mon–Wed, 12pm–2am; Thu, 12pm–12am; Fri–Sat, 12pm–3am; Sun, 12pm–11pm*

Ⓘ *Gourmet burger, £6.50*

Ⓩ *£9.75*

OTHER

The Basement Complex

7 Heaton's Court

(0113) 242 7730

Don't try and lie to us and say you never wished you were around in the heyday of Studio 54. Free love and funky music are things that are undeniably attractive to us all, but those good old days are long gone. So why not roll with it. Take your Simon Amstell style of gay and flip it over to reveal something a bit more Right Said Fred and float the night away in The Basement Complex. Sauna, steam room, large Jacuzzis, cinema rooms, beauty therapy and a café all in one fantastiche venue.

Ⓒ *Mon–Sun, 24 hours*

Ⓩ *£7–£12*

Velvet

11–12 Hirsts Yard

(0113) 242 5079

Now Itchy knows we're all beautiful people up North. Stunning, even, some of us. But at the end of it all there are those that are just unbelievably lucky in every department of life we can think of. They are happy, successful and gorgeous. They float along in their designer gear and laugh at each other's amazing jokes. Those people go here. So come along and learn, and see if you can persuade the beautiful people that you're one of them. It's an up-market place so be courteous. Oh, and maybe you ought to tip the velvet too, whatever that means.

Ⓒ *Mon–Sat, 12pm–12am; Sun, 12pm–10.30pm*

Xibit

24–32 Bridge End

(0113) 368 4648

Formerly The Base, Xibit is served up to us by Philip and Lance of The Bridge Inn. The old interior has been scooped out like an unwelcome dog poo and replaced with bright and bubbly décor, far from straight-laced vanilla. The venue also plays host to local artists' work and has been christened 'Leeds' only gay restaurant'. Open till 2am on the weekends and played out by DJs, it is possible to eat, drink and party in this one special place.

Ⓒ *Mon–Wed, 12pm–12am; Thu–Sat, 12pm–2am; Sun, 1pm–12.30am; Food, Sun, 1pm–5pm; Mon–Sat, 12pm–3pm & 5pm–8pm*

Ⓘ *Barbecue chicken, £7.95*

Ⓩ *£7.95*

Gay

CLUBS

The Birdcage

52–56 Boar Lane
(0113) 246 7273

Whether you think it's tacky or not, there's something just brilliant about watching drag shows. Not only does The Birdcage do cabaret, but they make it as fun and as naughty as any straight person can handle while giving the gay scene a place to camp it up to the limit. Watch out if it's your first time because you will leave the place wondering if everything you learnt at school about the human body and the way that it works was a load of bollocks… speaking of which…

🕒 *Wed–Thu, 9pm–2am; Fri–Sat, 8pm–3am; Sun, 9pm–1am*

SpeedQueen @ Rehab

Assembly Street
(0113) 244 9474

Since SpeedQueen packed up its worldly belongings and put them into an old flannel on the end of a stick, it has not looked back. Strutting along in a pair of cute vintage dungarees, wearing an old straw hat, whistling a happy, happy tune, kicking pebbles and picking daisies, Leeds' answer to the 'dressy up' night settles its boots on a Saturday night. It strips off its 'poor me' outfit and explodes in a fit of glam, flailing its every limb around in gigantic movements declaring 'Yo soy fabuloso – join me being fabuloso in Leeds'. And we reckon you should.

🕒 *Sat, 10pm–6am*
💷 £8/£10

Cabaret venues

It's just a stone's throw away from Manchester and a teeny weeny train ride from London but Leeds is establishing a pretty little gay scene for itself. From outrageous through stylish to screaming out loud about your happy gay life here's a the lowdown on where to start. **The Birdcage** (see above) is pure tack and glam with strippers and gorgeous girls and boys doing cabaret. Alternatively, check out **Club Federation** (www.clubfederation.com) at Fibre on Saturday nights. Sexy girls and hot guys writhing about in stylish next-to-nothing, surrounded by the buzz of funky music, it may not be billed as a cabaret but the dancers don't half put on a show. Don't forget **Pride** either (as if you could). Check out www.mesmac.co.uk for dates to hit the town with a pinch of glitter and a fist full of feathers.

SO YOU'RE A FRIEND OF DOROTHY WHO'S FOUND THEMSELVES IN A NEW TOWN, AND IT MIGHT AS WELL BE THE EMERALD CITY, YOU'RE SO CLUELESSLY GREEN. HOW DO YOU TRACK DOWN THE BEST PINK PLACES? LET ITCHY GUIDE YOUR RUBY SHOES WITH SOME PEARLS OF WISDOM…

Even if their tastes aren't quite yours, they can give you the lowdown on the more subtle gay haunts, and you and Toto will be going loco in no time.

Scally or pally? – Various gay fetishes for chav-style fashions can make

Gay abandoned

There's no place like homo – Just because you're out of the closet doesn't necessarily mean that you love the great outdoors; camping it up isn't for everyone. However, the most kitsch, flamboyant venues are generally well advertised and typically the easiest ones to find; their mass appeal means you usually get a fair old proportion of straights in there too, enjoying their recommended weekly allowance of cheese, but you should have no trouble tracking down a few native chatty scenesters.

it hard to tell a friendly bear pit from a threatening lions' den full of scallies, especially if you've only heard rumours that somewhere is a non-hetters' hot spot. Be cautious in places packed with trackies unless you want your Adid-ass kicked.

Get board – Internet message boards have honest, frequently updated tips; magazines like *Diva* and *Gay Times* have links to local forums on their sites. Click your mouse, not your heels, and get ready to go on a bender.

*Illustration by Si Clark
www.si-clark.co.uk*

gash.co.uk

gorgeous

adventurous

sexy

happening

lingerie & lovestuff

Gash Leeds
The Corn Exchange
Leeds LS1 7BR
0113 244 2214

Gash Sheffield
19 Westfield Terrace
Devonshire Qtr
Sheffield S1 4GH
0114 276 3733

Gash York
25 Fossgate
York YO1 9PA
01904 689 620

free gift wrap
24-hour mail delivery
salons & classes
own your own shop!

visit our stores or click on
our website for lingerie
& lovestuff
www.gash.co.uk

Shop

Shop

AREAS

Briggate and The Arcades

A shopping Mecca since 1752, Briggate is home to the swanky Harvey Nichols, where a man the same colour as a traffic cone in a top hat guards the doors. Under ornate covers, check out kooky gifts in Octopus, heaving, corsetted bosoms in Vivienne Westwood and all manner of boudoir frippery in Rose & Co. There are two Maccy Ds, so pick the closest one to avoid burning off valuable blubber as you waddle to the queue, or try German frikadellen instead from the mobile grill by Zara, followed by honeycomb, candyfloss or a Mr Whippy from the Childcatcher-style vans. Bag one of the highly coveted silver benches and spy on consumers while you consume.

The Corn Exchange
Call Lane
(0113) 234 0363

The Corn Exchange is at the heart of Leeds' alternative scene. From the glamorously chic Aqua Couture to the stylish vintage boutique Fabric Junkie and club-a-dub-dubbers Strawberri Peach, if you like your clobber with a twist then you'll find more excitement on these rails than a trainspotter on a Pendolino. Newly opened Gash sells gorgeous underwear and classy adult toys, while old favourite Yum Yum Beads stocks all you need to decorate other dangly bits with homemade jewellery. Stores like Grin are perfect for off-beat presents, whilst if it's off-beat presence you're seeking, go the hole way at Pro Body Piercing.

Speak easy

ITCHY'S GUIDE TO THE LOCAL LINGO

Leeds' global village status hasn't killed off the local dialect, known in these parts as Tyke. Indeed, you get a real sense that speaking like a Loiner is crucial to making sure that Leeds stays Leeds, and also to confuse anyone who's wandered here by mistake. If it's a bevvy you're after (and who isn't?), then Tyke comes into its own – you're advised to drink fast here – you must 'sozzle', 'guzzle' or 'gollop' your drink, but be careful, or you'll be 'drunk as fuzzocks'. Another word you'll probably think is simply there to confuse you is the strange use of the word 'while', in direct replacement for 'until'. So if you're wondering about that party invite which tells you it's 'on while 12', don't turn up fashionably late, as the party'll only be on 'til 12.

DEPARTMENT STORES

Debenhams

121 Briggate

(0113) 218 6300

Debenhams is now trying to appeal to people who still have their own teeth, with younger designers and concessions like Faith and Topshop alongside a vast cosmetics range and a choking number of perfume counters, but it just doesn't get our juices flowing. Itchy thinks they should do something radical to revive our interest, like rename it Deb 'n' Hams and have Paul Daniels' missus serving up sides of pork as she shimmers in her sequin dresses. We'd go then. As it stands, less than magical.

⦿ *Mon–Wed, 9.30am–6.30pm; Thu–Sat, 9.30am–7pm; Sun, 11am–5pm*

MEN'S CLOTHING

Mr Chimp

5 Thornton Arcade

(0113) 234 9979

Leeds – the urban jungle. Herds of switched-on busy shoppers stampede their way to the best bargains, leaving the average newcomer a little bemused. But away from the undergrowth of high street chains and the swarms of over-priced designer boutiques lies a little gem – and there ain't no monkey business about this place. Mr Chimp offers cool threads, bags of style, affordable price tags and a barrage of choice, all crammed into one rather tiny but perfectly formed shop. Who said the lion was king of the jungle?

⦿ *Mon–Sat, 10.30am–5.30pm*

House of Fraser

140–142 Briggate

(0113) 243 5235

House of Fraser has stepped up a gear over the last couple of years – probably something to do with the imposing shadow of Harvey Nic's looming a couple of doors away, shaking his cane in triumph across the cobbles and laughing maniacally as he strokes his Siamese cat. With brands like Diesel, Farhi, Mulberry and Carvela under his roof, our Fraser can at least dress smartly before he takes to the ring to confront big Nic in a celebrity department store death match, and thwaps him sharply about the chops with a neat pair of tailored suede driving gloves.

⦿ *Mon–Wed & Fri, 9am–5.30pm; Thu, 9am–7pm; Sat, 9am–6pm; Sun, 11am–5pm*

Shop

UNISEX CLOTHING

All Saints

33–35 Queen Victoria Street, Victoria Quarter
(0113) 243 2434

A staple shop for the Leeds brigade, meaning that although the threads you purchase will be mighty fine, you may find yourself in a 'Jesus Christ, they've got my belt on' saga, God forbid. However, this place is always worth a look (if only to see what cheaper knock-offs to look out for in Primark) and they hold probably the most heavenly sales on this earth, with prices slashed down as much as 70% by the hallowed blue cross. A saintly offering, wouldn't say?

ⓒ *Mon–Sat, 10am–6pm; Thu, 10am–7pm; Sun, 11am–5pm*

Primark

20 The Headrow
(0113) 245 7848

This bloated retail monstrosity now dwarfs the rest of the Headrow. You can buy about 15 new tops for your £1 pocket money. Fair play to Primark; with its democratic pricing, it's great for basics. However, for the right to buy your cheap-as-chips jeans, you're forced to rummage through near jumble-sale conditions, and wait long enough to grow some prize-winning facial hair as you queue for the changing rooms, and then the tills... At least that gives you time to observe those interesting fellows who appear to be attempting to pinch a pair of knickers that are already only 50p.

ⓒ *Mon–Sat, 9am–6pm; Thu, 9am–6pm; Sun, 11am–5pm*

Flannels

68–78 Vicar Lane
(0113) 234 9977

Über cool, über chic, über-sweetie-darling. More Prada graces these four walls (and three floors) than a New York catwalk during fashion week, and your wallet's guaranteed to purge its contents and slim down to a size 00. If money's already too tight to mention, you might be better off popping down the market and approximating the Flannels experience by purchasing a towelling facecloth. Which reminds us; one of Itchy's friends had an apartment above here where the tiles in the bathroom had jellybeans set into them. The sweetest-smelling loo in Leeds, surely.

ⓒ *Mon–Fri, 10am–6pm; Sat, 9.30am–6pm; Sun, 11am–5pm*

WOMEN'S CLOTHING

Aqua
36 Queen Victoria Street, Victoria Quarter
(0113) 243 3336

This place is worth a visit for the scorchio talent behind the counter alone, and on closer inspection it sells some pretty decent clobber too. Unfortunately, you'll need a stack of interest-free credit cards or a rich papa in order to purchase any of it. And a waist like a transparent stick insect during a famine viewed through the wrong end of a telescope after being shrunk on a boiling hot spin cycle; when it comes to the tight-fitting styles here, it's definitely aqua-stion of taut.

Ⓒ *Mon–Sat, 10am–6pm;*
Sun, 11.30am–4.30pm

Vicky Martin
42 Queen Victoria Street, Victoria Quarter
(0113) 244 1477

We've all suffered the 'mare of turning up at a do in the same outfit as someone else, eh ladies? But before you start throwing punch and punches, overturning crepe-paper bedecked buffet tables and hurling houmous around like the token bitch in a teen rom-com, stop! Vicky Martin can help. Purveyors of a better class of clubwear, all of their frocks are handmade and limited edition. Better still, they offer a great and relatively affordable bespoke design service. Start saving and sketching out your ideas now, and this party season you'll get to be the heroine for once. Vicky Martin – she bangs, you know.

Ⓒ *Mon–Sat, 10am–6pm; Sun, 12pm–5pm*

Boon Boutique
The Corn Exchange, Call Lane
(0113) 243 0363

Walking into Boon is like entering Barbie's boudoir. Hot pink assaults you from every angle. Big lovehearts flirt with you from the windows. There are even free sweets on offer. All of this caramel-drizzled, icing-dusted, chocolate-dipped whimsy may well be to distract you from the quality of the clothes, most of which are cheap and cheerful at best. If you're after fun but disposable fashion and are easily bribed with sugar, give the shop a look. If you're after something with timeless elegance, you'll find Boon Boutique about as much use as the contents of Ken's underpants.

Ⓒ *Mon–Sat, 10.30am–5.30pm;*
Sun, 11.30am–5.30pm

Shop

SECONDHAND

All Aboard

51 Otley Road

(0113) 278 7063

Often stocks genuine shipshape booty rather than just the usual secondhand pile of ship. While only a small place, the staff here have a magpie eye for kitsch tea sets and vintage picnic boxes, quirky handbags, art deco brooches, Mary Quant legwarmers, frothy prom dresses, and bow ties and braces enough to clothe your own chorus line. And while they they could hike the prices of such goodies higher than Simon Cowell's waistband, instead they still slouch lower than a thong-bearing slapper's muffin-topped joggers.

ⓦ *Mon–Fri, 9am–4pm; Sun, 11am–3pm*

Oxfam Originals

15–17 Duncan Street

(0113) 246 8486

Cheese fans can indulge in a CD rack jam-packed with Haddaway singles, and, erm, other cheese fans will be impressed with the variety of shoes on offer. Seriously, even if you've never before considered putting your feet where somebody else's have merrily sweated away, these well-preserved vintage one-offs may well tempt you to play footsie. Great clothes too, though sometimes actually quite pricey, so not always helpful if your bank balance is a charity case in itself. Serious book collectors and music enthusiasts should check out the specialist Headingley branch (13–15 Otley Road) for the ultimate in cheap thrills.

ⓦ *Mon–Sat, 9.30am–5pm; Sun, 11am–4pm*

Blue Rinse

11 Call Lane

(0113) 245 1735

A vintage boutique providing choicest retro to go, sparing you the odorous experience of scavenging through the charity shop mounds of Global Hypercolour T-shirts with stained armpits, cycling shorts with hairy strands of frayed lycra trailing from the crotch and crispy once-white, now-beige bras to uncover that leather jacket you've been lusting for. They do add on a couple of quid for the privilege, mind, but for your extra lolly you get to shop to an inspirational soundtrack and there's a selection of re-worked, recycled fashions to slip into as well. Rinsin'.

ⓦ *Mon–Sat, 10.30am–5.30pm; Sun, 11.30am–4.30pm*

SHOES

Dune

78 Briggate

(0113) 243 3872

Dune has won awards for its classic, top quality shoes and stocks matching handbags to accompany nearly every pair of heels. Even more reason to look where you're going – tread in a dog turd with these babies on and you'll never forgive yourself. Presumably why dune buggies were invented; so you can coast freely across parks, pavements, and beaches, high above the torrents of fetid canine effluent that might otherwise stain your luxury suede uppers with ostrich-effect tongue.

Mon–Fri, 9.30am–6pm; Sat, 9am–6pm; Sun, 11am–5pm

Size?

49–51 Vicar Lane

(0113) 243 2221

If you're after an obscure, original or limited edition trainer, Size? are your guys. From old skool basketball air-pocketed pump-ups in a collide-oscope of clashing colours to right on write-on sneakers that come with fabric markers to personalise them with, if you're searching for it, this lot will do all they can to ensure you're not de-feet-ed in your quest to invest. Head downstairs for cult and quirky sports brand clothing to match if you want to take your look a step further; they do a nice line in cheerleader-type satin skirts, new rave jumpsuits and unusually colour-coded Adidas jackets.

Mon–Wed, 9.30am–6pm; Thu–Sat, 9.30am–6.30pm; Sun, 11am–5pm

Puliga

176 Harrogate Road, Chapel Allerton

(0113) 269 6000

You'll wear your shoes out trekking all the way out of the city centre, handily justifying the purchase of a brand spanking new pair. And oh, how very brand and very spanking they shall be. Puliga aims to please, with a small but stunning selection of Italian and Spanish-made leathery lovelies to shove your stinking British plates of meat in. Prices are somewhat on the beefy side, but they offer an overnight lending service so you can take shoes home and check they match your outfits before you fork out a prime amount on luxury sties for your spoilt little piggies.

Mon–Wed, 9.30am–6pm; Thu–Sat, 9.30am–6.30pm; Sun, 11am–5pm

Shop

BOOKS

Blackwell's

21 Blenheim Terrace

(0113) 243 2446

You'll spot more students queueing in Blackwell's than you will in the local clap clinic after freshers' week. This university-linked book shop is as busy as a bookies on giro day around September time with first years pretending they're actually going to study. They have every book a hardworking student would ever need (so long as you get there early in the term) as well as loads of novels for those who actually enjoy reading. Plus they will buy the textbook back, at half price, when you've read the one chapter you bought it for.

☺ *Mon–Sat, 9am–5pm*

Waterstone's

36–38 Albion Street

(0113) 244 0839

The BFG of book shops. Waterstone's rains partially-digested snozzcumbers on the parade of its rivals, with exceptionally helpful staff and a splendid array of stock. There's a cosy café in case you can't wait until you get home to squidge crumbs of blueberry muffin deep down in the spine and stick pages 72–95 together with coffee froth, and they often have 3-for-2 offers on popular fiction to bury your matted head in, offering yet another diversion from the mundane tasks of the real world. Don't blame us if you start Shake 'n' Vac-ing your T-shirts and Febreeze-ing your pubes so you can spend your washing time reading.

☺ *Mon–Sat, 9am–6pm; Sun, 11am–5pm*

Borders

94–96 Briggate

(0113) 242 4400

With their unrivalled range of novelty, impulse-buy toys like Stewie-in-my-pockets, or the skin-crawlingly efficient 20Q that reads your mind, you may not have time to read all the cards in Paperchase, let alone pick up a book.

☺ *Mon–Sat, 9am–9pm; Sun, 11am–5pm*

WH Smith

3–7 Lands Lane

(0113) 242 2505

Is it a bookshop? Is it a stationer's? Is it a sweetshop? It's whatever you want it to be. So grab a pack of wine gums and a Mills and Boon and stop asking questions.

☺ *Mon, Wed–Fri, 8.45am–6pm; Tue, 9am–6pm; Sat, 11am–6pm; Sun, 11am–5pm*

MUSIC

HMV

1 Victoria Walk, Headrow Centre

(0113) 245 5548

Hum Music Vocally? Hit Music Video? Hike Mount Vesuvius? We'll guess right someday.

☺ *Mon–Sat, 9.30am–5.30pm; Sun, 10.30am–4.30pm*

Virgin

Albion Arcade, Albion Street

(0113) 243 8117

You may feel like a corporate whore for shopping here, but there are some days when all you want to do is froth at the mouth in a consumerist haze of spend, spend, spending.

☺ *Mon, 8am–6pm; Tue–Wed & Fri–Sat, 9am–6pm; Thu, 9am–7pm; Sun, 11am–5pm*

OTHER

The Condom Shop

Corn Exchange, Call Lane

(0113) 244 6532

Johnny rotten? Johnny be good – get out your johnny cash and get yourself down to this smut hut for a million flavours of misbehaviour in more shapes and sizes than anyone could shake their stick at. As well as helping you avoid contracting any unwelcome gifts from 'generous' partners, they stock a variety of kinky cards and perverse presents. If you are planning to (corn) exchange your bodily fluids, don't take a gamble; come to this johnny Vegas and win on every slot you play.

Ⓒ *Mon–Sat, 9.30am–5.30pm;*

Sun, 10.30am–4.30pm

Gash

Corn Exchange, Call Lane

(0113) 244 2214

The best erotic lifestyle store around? Corset is. Stocking the crème-de-la-crème in lingerie, toys, cosmetics and books, whether you're looking for something that holds AA boobs or AA batteries, Gash are sure to have it in its very sexiest sort. Classy not brassy, Itchy loves its 'personalised panties' embroidery service, and the free 'Gash Girls Nights' held on the first Wednesday of every month at Townhouse; expect talks, treats, and to want to do far more when you get home than simply take off your heels and order a meatfeast deep pan.

Ⓒ *Mon–Sat, 10.30am–5.30pm;*

Sun, 11am–4.30pm

Shop

Elm Street

Corn Exchange, Call Lane

(0113) 234 0363

Elm Street is piled with quirky film collectibles, mainly figures but with posters and T-shirts on offer too. The selection is impressive and obviously sourced with much love. Most items aren't cheap but would make a great present for that special dweeb in your life, for this is a geek speakeasy. Casual browsers beware: laughing in this cathedral of kookiness is not recommended. Staff will punish you with a spine-chilling glare, and you may well be tortured in the night with obscure sci-fi box sets and director commentaries. Now that's what Itchy calls a nightmare.

© *Mon–Fri, 10am–5.30pm;*
Sat, 9.30am–6pm; Sun, 11am–4pm

Hippypottermouse

Corn Exchange, Call Lane

(0113) 467 265

The most old age new age shop in Leeds, in that it's been around seemingly since the dawn of time. Entertainingly mythical and mystical, from incantations and potions to tarot card readings and fair trade clothing, this place has got the lot. They stock books on the subject of love spells, in case your partner's wand has lost its magic: peace out with your piece out. Hippypottermouse is a mobile phone-free zone too, further protecting your virility from semen-zapping Siemens and ensuring that your pleasant browse through instructions on how to brew up passion with sulphur and toads' eyes isn't ruined by the Crazy Frog.

© *Mon–Sat, 9.30am–5.30pm*

Org Organics

79 Great George Street

(0113) 234 7000

Organic, ethical foods, household products and cosmetics together with a café and a range of holistic treatments. Claiming to be a completely sustainable operation, Org recycle waste, re-use carrier bags and even plant trees to offset the carbon emissions caused by their delivery service. With stylish surroundings, great products and a guilt-free shopping experience, Org is guaranteed to get you glowing inside and out. Forget crusty stereotypes – this is a retailer that goes against the grain. Plus the name reminds Itchy of the band Orange Organics from old kids' series *Pugwall*.

© *Mon–Fri, 9.30am–5.30pm;*
Sat, 9.30am–5pm; Sun, closed

IF YOU THINK VEGGIES ARE CRANKY, YOU'LL LOVE THIS. FREEGANS SAY OUR ECONOMIC SYSTEM HURTS THE ENVIRONMENT, TREATS ANIMALS CRUELLY AND WORKERS UNFAIRLY, AND WASTES RESOURCES, SO YOU SHOULDN'T PAY FOR FOOD. IDIOTS. HERE'S HOW WE'D BE FREEGANS…

1. Have a Pret dinner – The bods who run Pret a Manger obviously don't know much about the principles of Freeganism, given how much they throw away each day. Turn up at closing, rummage through their bin bags, and hey presto – free dinner.

2. Kill an animal – Apparently it's legal for you to kill squirrels on your own property. With this in mind, set up a bird table, cover it in superglue and get the pot boiling while you wait for it to become a squirrel lolly. Sure, you might snare the odd bird, but extra protein's always welcome, and the RSPB'll never catch you.

3. Forage – Those in the country could nick apples from trees and scour woodland floors for wild mushrooms. Alternatively, those of us whose parents aren't blood-related to each other could pull half-eaten trays of late-night chips from bins.

4. Mug a milkman – Those bastards don't need all that milk. But you do. Being a freegan isn't conducive to a calcium-rich diet, after all. Wait until your local milky's delivering to a dark area, then knock him out and chug as many bottles as you can before making your getaway.

5. Sniper rifle the zoo – Get up high, and train your gun on the elephant cage. It's not going to be easy to take one of those suckers down with one shot, but if it pays off, you'll be eating like a monarch for weeks. Plus you could sell the tusks on to practitioners of Chinese medicine for extra cash.

Freegan fun

Illustration by Thomas Denbigh

0800700200
FREE
PHONE

G.A.N
SKIP HIRE

www.freegan.info

AA | driving school

enjoy

Buy 2 AA driving lessons and get 1 FREE*.

Don't miss out! Book your first lesson today.
Call 0800 107 2044.

www.AAdrivingschool.co.uk

AA driving school. Drive your dreams forward

FREE
AA DRIVING LESSON

Your FREE AA driving lesson voucher

Book your first lessons today.
Call 0800 107 2044. Buy 2 lessons, then simply hand this voucher to your AA driving instructor at your first lesson to arrange your free lesson.

Your Name	**(Instructor use only)** AA Driving Instructor Name

Your Pupil Number	AA Driving Instructor Number

(Given on calling 0800 107 2044)

*Offer closes 31st March 2008. Only 1 free hour of tuition will be given per pupil. Offer not available to existing AA driving school pupils and cannot be used in conjunction with any other offer. Offer subject to instructor availability. AA driving instructors are self-employed franchisees and all contracts for the provision of driving tuition are between the pupil and the instructor. Only one voucher redeemable per pupil. Full terms and conditions are available at www.AAdrivingschool.co.uk

Code 342 – Itchy

Out & about

Out & about

CINEMAS

Hyde Park Picture House

Brudenell Road

(0113) 275 2045

Originally a hotel, the Picture House screens a variety of independent, art-house, classic and foreign films, with regular themed movie marathons. Itchy remembers when Snickers used to be called Marathons, and the advert had some rocker bloke who played his guitar more fervently when the voiceover offered him 'more nuts'. With cheap tickets, original gas lighting and a decorated Edwardian balcony, we're nuts for this place. Seek Hyde.

🕒 *Doors open: Fri, 6pm;*
Sat, 12pm; Sun, 4pm
💷 *£4–£4.50*

Vue

22 The Light, The Headrow

(08702) 403 696

Vue is a typical chain cinema; it's all endless escalators and bright lights like an airport corridor, and you'll have to wait until some little old lady you donated tins of creamed sweetcorn to from the back of your cupboard at harvest festival 1983 remembers you in her will before you can afford the pic 'n' mix. And even the you'd avoid the heavy jelly snakes. If shelling out a fiver for some syrupy H_2O with extra CO_2 leaves you struggling for breath, O2 is not the answer – grab a friend on an Orange tariff instead and head down on a Wednesday for the two for one ticket deal.

🕒 *Times vary*
💷 *Adults, £6.25*

COMEDY CLUBS

Jongleurs
The Cube, Albion Street
(08707) 870 707

Comedy, food, drink. What more could you ask for? Two dance floors, a lounge area and several bars? Cor blimey mate, you drive a hard bargain; tell you what, we'll sort that out for you, but only if we can allow stag and hen nights to flock here by the bus-load, so you'll be forced to wear an L-plate and fairy wings if you don't want to look out of place. Deal? We'll chuck in the smell of stale fag smoke to curb your enjoyment of cheap food during daylight hours at adjoining Bar Risa too.

🕒 *Thu–Sat from 8pm (dance floor 'til 2am)*
🎟 *From £8*

The House of Fun
Upstairs at The Original Oak, Otley Road, Headingley
(0113) 275 1322

Waking up on a Friday morning with a dirty hangover and face ache generally means Itchy has done something really regrettable with Clammy Clive. This time, we were relieved to remember that we'd simply let him take us to The House Of Fun. Our jaw muscles hurt merely from laughing so much at the great comedians and downing a whole lot of cheap booze in cosy surroundings that not even Clive managed to make feel uncomfortable. We still brushed our teeth really thoroughly though, just in case.

🕒 *Thu, 8pm–11pm*
🎟 *£4.89*
🎫 *£5*

Let's get physical

Keeping fit: it can be fun. Don't believe us? Mosey on down to **Yorkshire Dance** (3 St Peters Buildings, 0113 243 8765). Classes range from African Caribbean to Street Dance, and everything in between. Guaranteed to get your heart pumping, your booty shakin' and your calories burning. Classes will cost you the same as a Big Mac meal. No prizes for guessing which is the better way to spend your lolly. Feeling a little bit saucy? For those more, ahem, sensual among us, **Atrium** (6 Grand Arcade, 0113 242 6116), offers weekly pole dancing lessons every Monday night. Taught by their resident pole dancing experts, it's a sure-fire way to make your calf muscles ache and keep your significant others grinning from ear to ear all at the same time.

Out & about

THEATRES

Grand Theatre and Opera House

46 New Briggate

(0113) 222 6222

He's behind you! Oh no he isn't! Oh yes he is! Quick, run away to the freshly refurbed Grand and hide at a panto, or if it's not Christmas, take refuge in a musical, comedy, or one of Opera North's warblingly wonderful productions, and hope that some day the police will take your requests for an injunction against the creepy guy who's followed you from Morrisons fish counter seriously. Until then, this is a highly entertaining place to escape to.

🕐 *Times vary*

🕐 *£8.50–£50*

Leeds City Varieties Music Hall

Swan Street

(0113) 243 0808

An 18th century music hall which some would say is still stuck in the 18th century, largely due to its emphasis is on pleasing people that were born in the 18th century. Well, not quite that far back, but with acts such as Tom O'Connor, Freddie Starr and Ken Dodd, don't go expecting the Pussy Cat Dolls. It just won't happen. Mind you, they have had Russell Brand and Vashti Bunyan, so we suppose it's like a tin of Fox's Variety biscuits; there's some tempting creamy types in there, but also the ones everyone wants to leave.

🕐 *Doors open 7pm*

🕐 *£6–£15*

Half an hour of fun

Got half an hour to kill? Want a quick coffee without the pang of guilt you feel at supporting Starbucks? **Art's Cafe** (42 Call Lane, 0113 243 8243) has a great, laid-back atmosphere and does the most excellent hot chocolates. The selection of tunes at **Jumbo Records** (St John's Centre, 0113 245 5570) makes for great browsing if you're after something slightly less mainstream. If this is a shop you've never been in, take a look. There's the **Maumoniat International Food Supermarket** (35–43 Brudenell Grove, 0113 278 2432), too. With a mouth-watering selection of foods, this place is a whistle-stop gastronomic world tour. Or, if you prefer more artificial flavours, try **The Condom Shop** (Corn Exchange, 0113 244 6532). A bit of smut never harmed anyone.

MUSEUMS

The National Museum of Photography, Film and Television

Bradford

(08707) 010 200

Sitting on your arse watching re-runs of *Noel Edmonds' Telly Addicts* and wincing when you get a sharp bit of Dorito stuck in your throat is officially art. This was recognised when Bradford built a museum in homage to the VIP that is TV, along with the noble mediums of film and photography. It's home to an IMAX screen and three million items of cultural value (three million and one when Itchy comes to visit).

🕐 *Tue–Sun, 10am–6pm*

🎟 *Free; booking advised for cinema*

Thackray Medical Museum

Beckett Street

(0113) 244 4343

The 'Empathy Belly' here lets blokes know what it feels like to be up the duff, like Arnie learned for real in *Junior*, bearing Emma Thompson's seed. Wandering round the 'Pain, Pus and Blood' exhibition after a night on the tiles, Itchy's green-tinged face already clearly demonstrated how our own stomachs felt watching a re-enaction of a girl having her leg amputated while enduring a hangover. We were enduring the hangover, not her. Although if someone was about to hack us up below the knee with a Black & Decker, we'd feel entitled to a stiff drink too.

🕐 *Mon–Sun, 10am–5pm (last entry 3pm)*

🎟 *Adults, £4.90; concs £3.90; parking, £1*

Royal Armouries

Armouries Drive

(0113) 220 1916

History lessons always had potential to be fun; all those grisly details about ducking stools and kiddies getting their hair ripped off in spinning machines. Sadly, Itchy just seemed to spend a lot of time being forced to draw endless diagrams about crop rotation. The Royal Armouries gives you three thousand years of history taught way you want it; perfect for those Sundays when you feel like doing more than watching the *Hollyoaks* omnibus, and absolutely no mention of Jethro Tull's seed drill.

🕐 *Every day, 10am–5pm except Christmas Eve and Christmas Day*

🎟 *Free entry; however, some activities and events may be chargeable*

Tropical World

Canal Gardens, Roundhay Park

(0113) 266 1850

The polka dot puffer; nope, not the latest incentive to make asthma inhalers fashionably sexy, or something donated to Scope by Two Hats from Goldie Lookin' Chain (and then bought back after their record label dropped them), but in fact one of Tropical World's kooky aquarium inhabitants that happily co-exist with over 40 different varieties of butterfly and the only monkey in the world that comes out to play at night. Yes, there's only one. That spanking species doesn't count.

🕐 *Mon–Sun, 10am–6pm (last admission 5.30pm)*

🎟 *Adults, £3; kids (8–15yrs), £2*

Out & about

GALLERIES

Henry Moore Institute

74 The Headrow
(0113) 234 3158

Whether you're feeling artsy on a whim, or are a hardened sculpture enthusiast, this place is Moore than worth a trip. We all have a touch of the culture vulture inside us you know – unleash the beast here and let it feed. The award-winning retro-futuristic black marble building often has images projected onto it at night, and for a while broadcast the sound of running water, forcing Itchy to have to do an emergency pee up against it every time we walked past. Sorry Henry.

Ⓒ *Mon–Sat, 10am–5pm; Wed, 10am–8pm; closed Bank Holidays*

Salts Mill

Shipley, Saltaire
(01274) 531 185

This place first opened in 1853 as a textiles mill where kiddies worked the looms until their fingers were worn down to the length of their toes, and their spines had more humps than Abi Titmuss. In 1987 it was transformed into three floors of art, music, books, flowers, shops and a better-than-the-rest restaurant, Salts Diner. Admission is free; you can have run of the mill for nowt, so any penny pincher worth their salt and should go and take a gander. Or a goose. Itchy hears that art galleries are impressive places to bring birds.

Ⓒ *Mon–Fri, 10am–5.30pm; Sat–Sun, 10am–6pm*

Ⓕ *Free*

Leeds City Art Gallery

The Headrow
(0113) 247 8248

If what you know about contemporary canvases doesn't span much further than Tony Hart trying to get excited about yet another toddler's Pritt-Stick effort shedding lentils and bits of dried spaghetti all over the studio floor, then this place could Morph your education up a grade. Showing that you don't need to go to London to view the greats, Leeds City has housed some pretty almighty exhibitions alongside a decent permanent collection including Rembrandt and Bridget Riley. There should be more than enough here to make even the most uncultured art beat faster.

Ⓒ *Mon–Sat, 10am–5pm; Wed, 10am–8pm; Sun, 1pm–5pm*

LIVE MUSIC

The Cockpit
Swinegate
(0113) 244 1573

Despite its name, those who frequent this place generally keep their dangly bits below their belts rather than attached to their foreheads; there's no pretension, next to no light and not many places who do it better. If you're after indie or music with rocks in, come here to catch carefully selected acts raising the under-the-arches roof in an atmosphere more intimate and intense than a bikini wax. Keep the wardrobe dark if you don't want to stand out like the Queen at a cattle market.

ⓘ *Gigs from 7.30pm*
ⓔ £4–£16

Joseph's Well
Chorley Lane
(0113) 203 1861

With gigs every night of the week and recent appearances by The Killers, Keane, Buck 65, Kaiser Chiefs, Bloc Party, The Kills, The Stills, The Dears, Send More Paramedics, iLiKETRAiNS and Lars Frederecksen, this place is fierce. A bit shabby round the edges, with carpets sponsored by Evostick, but all the more real for it. Entry to the bar is free and gigs are cheaper than deep fried slices of starchy root vegetable, so you can afford to take a chance on someone you've never heard of. Chuck a fiver down the Well, make a musical wish, and it will probably be granted.

ⓘ *Gigs from 7pm*
ⓔ £3–£7

The HiFi Club
2 Central Road
(0113) 247 7353

The live equivalent of sticking your headphones in during a break at work. You know, those escapist moments when you drown out the office with something suitably mellow or ragingly cathartic. The music helps repair that bit of your soul withered by being ordered to hard-sell more boiler insurance to innocent grannies by someone who wears a Cliff Richard T-shirt on dress down Fridays. HiFi is your saviour, offering jazz, funk, rock and friendship in a world that doesn't understand we don't all want to live in an electro-house.

ⓘ *Mon–Wed, 10pm–2am;*
Thu, 10pm–2.30am; Fri, 10pm–3am;
Sat, 7pm–3am; Sun, 12pm–12.30am

Out & about

Leeds Metropolitan University Students Union
Calverly Street
(0113) 283 2600

The LMUSU (as you must call it – say 'Leeds Met' or 'Leeds Met Union' and they'll pretend not to understand) is a fantastic venue which showcases some of the hottest acts around. Leeds Uni does put up a damned good fight; however, Itchy saw DJ Shadow shamefully forced to perform next to posters of roast chickens in their refectory 5 years back, and despite extensive refurbs since, we just can't shake the feeling that the Met has the edge on this one. Check out their lovely pink website for gig details at www.leedsmetevents.co.uk.

🕒 Times vary
💷 From £6

STRIP CLUBS

Buffalo Lounge
68 New Briggate
(0113) 244 6161

Buff 'ello indeed, to stunning, classy hostesses from across the world. This gentlemen's club is 'more about complete entertainment' than straight up-and-down pole dancing; as if the ladies' wiggling and jiggling wasn't diversion enough, they lay on DJs, belly dancing and comedians (the 'butt' of all comic 'strip' jokes – arf), and claim to be the first northern venue to host professional burlesque tease evenings. Splash out on some champers, and prepare to say 'Phwoar' to Buffalo. You herd.

🕒 Mon–Sun, 8pm–6am
💷 From £10

The Packhorse
208 Woodhouse Lane
(0113) 245 3980

This place made its name as a convenient stop on the Otley run and not as a great venue. Mediocre bands coupled with horribly sweaty clientele can be the order of the night, so sometimes you'd be better off ordering a dirty kebab instead of staying at home. However, make definite exception for anything organised by Leeds On The Bone – these experts have fingers in a lot of baby pies in Leeds that grow up to be big tasty meaty ones, and they often give out free CDs too. They turn The Packhorse from donkey to stallion. Check event listings online: www.leedsonthebone.com.

🕒 Gigs from 7pm
💷 £2–£5

SPORT

Goals Five-a-side Football

Redcote Lane (off Kirkstall Road)

(0113) 263 0303

Goals is Leeds' stand-out venue for the mini version of the beautiful game, thanks to its superbly organised evening leagues, lovely surface, referees and online results, tables and stats. They've cornered the market for competitive league matches and judging by the frequent price hikes, they know it, although this hasn't so far proved to be an own goal as the punters keep a-comin'. If you're after a more leisurely kick about, pitches are also available for hire at South Leeds Stadium, Soccer City in Beeston, Beckett Park and local leisure centres.

€ Pitch hire, £36.75

Headingley Cricket Ground

Headingley Carnegie Stadium, St Michaels Lane

(0113) 278 7394

If, for you, cricket conjures up images of gentle ripples of applause from men in knotted hankies, cucumber sandwiches in Tupperware boxes and the *Daily Telegraph* blowing in the wind, then you're not far wrong. Unless you're a cricket nut, your best bet is to seek out the Twenty20 Cup games and England internationals (booking tickets in advance is essential). Both provide guaranteed sell-outs, top entertainment and plenty of high jinks amongst the intoxicated revellers on the 'notorious' Western Terrace. Get the strawberries in, press your slacks, and watch the good old boys thwap it, righto?

€ Adults, from £15

Out & about

Leeds Rhinos – Rugby League

Headingley Carnegie Stadium, St Michaels Lane
(0113) 278 6181

'Get Horny!' is Leeds Rhinos' marketing slogan. Although actual physical arousal is probably pushing it a bit, this is definitely the place to come if you like your action dirty, fast and hard. Blokes with necks the same girth as old oaks stick their heads up each other's arses with only passing interest in the whereabouts of the ball, and don't the locals love it? Last year was unusually barren for the Rhinos but Headingley's finest will be looking to put that right this time around. Mayhem comes in pint glasses at the Skyrack and Original Oak afterwards.

❸ Adults, £16–£30

Leeds Tykes – Rugby Union

Headingley Carnegie Stadium, St Michaels Lane
(0845) 0700 881

Watching the Leeds Tykes has lost a bit of its glamour since their relegation to National League One, but hard core egg-chasers will still find 80 minutes of distraction here for them every other weekend. Perhaps they should increase their revenue and buy some better players by launching an exciting new range of fan merchandise alongside the shirts; they could have Tykes Nikes, Tykes bikes, Tykes trikes, sponsored Tykes hikes, Tykes Dy...hmmm, maybe not, although it would bring an interesting new derogatory inference to the phrase 'rugger bugger'.

❸ Adults, £14–£16

Leeds United FC

Elland Road
(08451) 211 992

The club's rousing anthem 'Marching on together, We're gonna see you win', is sung more in desperate hope than expectation these days by the ever-dwindling home crowds down Beeston way. With glorious memories of Alan Smith scoring the clincher away to Lazio in the Champions League still fresh, watching the washed-out Whites struggle to break down Colchester in the Championship makes Itchy want to sob. But the good times won't return without a bit of faith, so mop up the tears, turn up and sing up. Who knows, this season we might even finish above Plymouth. Geographically.

❸ Adults, £21–£46

Swim & Gym

Leeds City Council Leisure Centres

(0113) 214 5088

All Leeds City Council leisure centres allow you unlimited access to any fitness class, gym or swimming session if you get yourself a snappily named Bodyline card, which sounds uncannily like a retro range of spraypump gels by Wella. If Itchy's body had a line, it certainly wouldn't have been drawn with a ruler, sporting a few more bumps than we'd prefer and probably reading something like 'We love pork pies, us, especially the salty jelly and the white lardy chunks'. Throw your wobbly bits away by working up some perspiration pumping iron, and then share your rancid bodily fluid with everyone else by diving into the pool. Marvellous.

OTHER

Meanwood Valley Urban Farm

Sugarwell Road, Meanwood

(0113) 262 9759

If city life is getting you down and you long for the comforts of stroking and cuddling something a bit fluffier and sweeter-smelling than your other half, then head down to Meanwood. It's only a short distance from the city centre, but you do feel as if you're in the middle of the countryside, and the experience is a hell of a lot more pleasant than being chased through a muddy field by a bloody big bull on a Duke of Edinburgh Award expedition.

🕒 *Open all year round*

🎫 *Adults, £1*

Tennis and Squash Courts

Wensley Avenue, Chapel Allerton

(0113) 226 6622

Indisputably the classiest place to swing a racket. It's members only, but the fees aren't jaw-dropping and you'll not find better facilities or more enthusiastic, well-organised clientele in all our green and pleasant land. There are leagues and teams for every standard (even Itchy's, which is somewhere below 'bog' and hovering around 'sub'), indoor, hard and grass courts for tennis and five courts for squash. And a bar, stocking proper pints alongside those worryingly neon energy drinks that make your pee glow in the dark so you can see if you're missing the bowl when you get up for a wizz in the night. Handy.

🕒 *Mon–Sun, 7am–11pm*

Roundhay Park

Roundhay Road, Roundhay

(0113) 266 1850

Absolutely spot on for something other than the usual rubbish to throw a weekend away on, –Roundhay Park has three different gardens and the endlessly fascinating Tropical World (see page 91), plus it hosts great live concerts and the best Bonfire Night ever. One of Itchy's mates had a girlfriend nicknamed the Roundhay Fox after the pub nearby. She wasn't bad looking, but it was more that odd habit she had of rifling through bins looking for scraps of discarded doner meat and congealed lamb bhuna.

🕒 *Mon–Sun, dawn–dusk;*

🎫 *Free except for special events, when prices vary*

Out & about

Xscape

Colorado Way, Glasshoughton, Castleford
(08712) 003 221

Ever thought you'd be coursing down the slopes in Leeds? No, we don't need professional Alp; this place has real, 100% butt-freezing snow. Skiing, snowboarding and sledging, alongside climbing walls, bowling lanes, a multi-screen cinema, interactive games, cafés, restaurants, some great shops and the chance to rediscover at least 3 old mix tapes on your car stereo when you get stuck in traffic trying to get out again. Itchy takes no responsibility for the fact that you remember all the words to Ace of Base's *All That She Wants*.

◉ *Mon–Sat, 9am–11.30pm;*
Sun, 10am–11pm
◉ *Prices vary*

Yorkshire Sculpture Park

West Bretton, Wakefield
(01924) 832 631

500 acres of 18th century parkland packed full of modern and contemporary art, most of it large enough to save you from being involuntarily cryogenically frozen by shielding you from Leeds' typically blustery weather. A day here thus makes a good windy break and way to break wind when you're feeling arty farty. Even if your knowledge of sculptures isn't your trump card, the park itself is a scenic paradise. Take a picnic, head down to the lake, and enjoy the beauty you never even knew was there. It will blow you away.

◉ *Mon–Sun, 10am–5pm*
◉ *Free except for special events,*
when prices vary

Stag & hen

Illustration by Thomas Denbigh

TAKE YOUR PECK FROM ITCHY'S ALTERNATIVE HEN IDEAS OR THROW A SIMPLY STAGGERING STAG DO. WELL, STAGGERING IS SURE TO BE INVOLVED SOMEWHERE ALONG THE LINE…

Unless the bride/groom's into the type of swinging that doesn't happen in park play areas (if it does – hell, you need to move to a better estate), by saying 'I do' your friend is promising not to indulge in bratwurst boxing with anyone but their chosen partner. For £52 per person, you can make sure they pack in the porking prior to the big day at a sausage-making course (www.osneylodgefarm.co.uk), and fry up the results the morning after to calm your hangovers.

As they're already selflessly donating themselves to someone else for life, chuck some extra charity in the mix; if you can raise enough cash for a good cause, experiences like bungee jumping, fire walking and skydiving are absolutely free. Wedding guests could pledge sponsorship as part of their gifts to the couple, and the money saved could go towards an extra few days on the honeymoon. Suitable charities for those getting hitched to munters include the Royal National Institute of the Blind or Battersea Dogs' Home.

Laters

Food

There are that many takeaways in Leeds that it's hard to even attempt to find you the best. So a fail-safe that does almost everything is Café De Niro's (44–46 New York Street, 0113 243 0111), offering the works, from filled Yorkshires to ice cream, and it's open 'til 4am Sunday to Thursday, and 'til 4.30am the rest of the week. For a tried and trusted Chinese, call Shanghai (Hyde Park, 0113 274 8020); the satay sauce is awesome and they're known for delivering your supper in super quick time.

Cigarettes

There are few things worse on this earth than realising that you're clean out of tabs after normal shop closing. Thank God then, for good old 24-hour garages, those bastions of 4am smoking sanity. The Shell (217 Kirkstall Road, 0113 242 8384) on Kirkstall Road is the place to buy your late-night smokes, skins and munchies. Oh, and De Niro's (see left) sells them too.

Alcohol

Pulled? Party dying down? Just finished work? Beer goggles slipping off? Bored? Drowning your sorrows? Celebrating? Just got home after a late flight from holiday? All-nighter for an essay and need inspiration? Itchy can think of any excuse for alcohol to be available throughout

the night and we're glad to give you a few places that will sell it to you at any time. Tesco's 24-hour store (361 Roundhay Road, 0113 214 7400) is licensed around the clock due to a change in the law, as is ASDA (Killingbeck Drive, 0113 249 9004), which is open from 8am on Monday 'til 10pm on Saturday.

Relax

Gone are the days of spiritual healing being reserved for the kooky and weird; we've finally found something legal that makes us feel as light as a piece of popcorn. At Just Float (64 North Street, 0113 243 3800), for £32 you get to go in a room of your own, strip, lie in a giant egg and float away

for an hour. Super salty water keeps you hovering and you can choose to be in complete darkness and silence, which is well worth the fear.

Late night shopping

So, the story goes that you go to work every day to earn money. You earn your money to be able to live a good life, eat out, enjoy drinks with friends, personal grooming and shopping. The problem there is that while you're out working for your hard-earned pennies, the shops are full of those who either get their money from elsewhere or are simply born with it... Jealous? Us? Never. So here's your guide to the havens of late night consumer indulgence in

Late licences

If you're one of the many Leeds night crawlers, head over to the rightfully popular **Normans** to strut among the beauties and drink 'til 3 or 4am. If you listen to your liver and not your head, you could brave **Townhouse** for a quick sip. Chock full of footballers and rugby players, this warehouse turned bar-club serves until 4.30am on a Saturday night. It's a veritable posing pouch of people who

like to see and be seen, mind, so avoid if you prefer things more relaxed. If you're still in the mood for mixing, wobble your way to the newly refurbished **Club Mission**. It hosts three dark, laser-filled rooms and an outside terrace (suitable for getting a bit of air), and stays open 'til 9am, meaning it can to be your last stop, besides that café you're going to next to chow down a fry-up.

Leeds. The White Rose (Dewsbury Road, 0113 229 1234) is open 'til 9pm on Thursdays and Harvey Nichols (111 Briggate, 0113 204 8888) and The Light (The Headrow, 0113 218 2060) are open 'til 8pm, so there's no excuse for clogging up the walkways on a Saturday.

Fun and games

Remember Quasar? Remember dodgems and bowling and prizes and everything? Lucky for us the carnies stayed in town and built a massive house for all our childhood faves. Well, LA Bowl (Sweet Street, 0808 108 5252) isn't exactly a proper fair but it's sparkly, brash and bright, with a DJ playing all of the cheesy music

you could wish for. The best thing is that it's open 'til 11pm midweek, and at weekends 'til much later.

Sheesha

Fancy relieving stress or a chilled out night with friends? Whether you're a smoker or not, the different flavours of tobacco available are unreal, from bubble gum to double apple. Roll up to Kadas (3 Crown Street, 0113 243 3433) to enjoy a smoke. It's open 'til 5am Fri–Sat, and 'til 4am the rest of the time. Alternatively get one delivered from De Niro's (see p104) at £15 for a baby or £25 for a big one. Flavoured tobacco starts from £3.50, and you can get hold of those little bits of coal from 30p each.

Fun @ night

DON'T WASTE THE GIFT OF INSOMNIA BY COUNTING IMAGINARY ANIMALS – GO CREATE SOME SHEAR (ARF) MAYHEM IN THE EARLY AM AND ENTER THE ITCHY TWILIGHT ZONE. WE WOOL IF YOU WOOL

Go jousting – First up, feed up for some insane-sbury's prices. As witching hours approach, 24-hour supermarkets reduce any unsold fresh produce to mere coppers; pick up a feast for a few pauper's pennies and buy them clean out of 10p French sticks, which are spot on for sword fights. Up the ante by jousting using shopping trolleys or bicycles in place of horses, or start a game of ciabatta-and-ball by bowling a roll.

Play street games – Take some chalk to sketch a marathon hopscotch grid down the entire length of the thoroughfare, or an anaconda-sized snakes and ladders board writhing across your town square. Break the trippy silence and deserted stillness of the dead shopping areas with a tag, catch or British bulldog competition, and be as rowdy as you like – there's no-one around to wake.

Illustration by Thomas Denbigh

Play Texaco bingo – Alternatively, drive the cashier at the all-night petrol station honey nut loopy by playing Texaco bingo: the person who manages to make them go back and forth from the window the most times to fetch increasingly obscure, specific and embarrassing items wins. Along with your prize-winning haul of mango chutney-flavoured condoms, Tena Lady towelettes and tin of eucalyptus travel sweets, be sure to pick up a first-edition paper to trump everyone over toast with your apparently psychic knowledge of the day ahead's events-to-be. Whatever you do, remember: you snooze, you lose.

Book cut-price, last minute accommodation with Itchy Hotels

Itchy Hotels has a late booking database of over 500,000 discount hotel rooms and up to 70% off thousands of room rates in 4-star and 5-star hotels, bed and breakfasts, guesthouses, apartments and luxury accommodation in the UK, Ireland, Europe and worldwide.

hotels.itchycity.co.uk

or book by phone: 0870 478 6317

Sleep

Sleep

SWANKY

42 The Calls
42 The Calls
(0113) 244 0099
Popular with the fashionable bar mules, this is the place to stay to see Leeds in the most stylish of company.
Rooms, from £105

The Queen's
City Square
(0113) 243 1323
Conveniently next to the train station, The Queen's is pure luxury inside and out. Make a good impression by sending your folks here when they come to stay – in a room with separate beds of course (urgh).
Rooms, from £89

Quebecs
9 Quebec Street
(0113) 244 8989
If you're planning on taking someone special for a night of utter luxury you haven't read as far as the next review, you'll want to book a room at Quebecs. Everything you'd expect from a 5 star stay, and more.
Rooms, from, £99

Residence6
The Old Post Office, City Square
(0113) 285 6250
If daddy's loaded and coming to visit, book him in here – this is the place to live it up in Leeds if you like it swanky. If not, take a look at the website and give yourself a goal in life. Un-funkin-believable.
Rooms, from £150–£475

MID-RANGE

Bewley's
City Walk
(0113) 234 2340
It's like an Ikea you can sleep in without having to hide in a wardrobe 'til everyone's gone home, but with better food and nicer staff.
Rooms, from £69

Haley's Hotel and Restaurant
8 Shire Oak Road
(0113) 278 4446
It's hard to explain in words just how attractive this listed building is. We think 'wow' is about as close as we can get. This is one of those proper cosy-home hotels with a warm welcome and real food.
Rooms, from £65

Ibis
Marlborough Street
(0113) 220 4100
Smack bang in the middle of the centre, and for the price of an Xbox game, it's hard to find a reason not to stay here. It may be basic in the décor but the wifi internet access will keep you too busy to notice.
Rooms, from £50

Moorlea Hotel
146 Woodsley Road
(0113) 243 2653
Cheap and crammed, with super-friendly owners and staff. One of those house-turned-B&B efforts. If you've got friends over and haven't got room for them among the beer bottles and pizza boxes, send 'em here.
Rooms, from £44

CHEAP

The Butlers Hotel

40 Cardigan Road

(0113) 274 4755

Sick of being treated like a slave? Run away from the mansion, leave your former life and master behind and check in here.

Rooms, from £10

Highbank Hotel

83 Harehills Lane

(0113) 262 2164

A massive house located in its very own grounds where you can get a room at pauper's prices. Blimey guvnor, what a treat. Take some time out and relax before hitting the city to spend the money you saved.

Rooms, from £38

Roomzzz Central

2 Burley Road

(0113) 233 0400

Ok. If it's not a hotel, then what the hell is it? Well, this is one of those serviced apartment jobbies, catering for those that spend months on end or even just the odd night in Leeds for work or play.

Rooms, from £35

Travelodge

Blayds Court, off Swingate, (08701) 911 655

97 Vicar Lane, (08701) 911 837

Golden chain for pennywise voyagers who still fancy a bed that doesn't feel like it's made of nails. Bagloads better value than similarly situated establishments. Don't bodge it – Lodge it.

Rooms, from £26

'The tables here are cleaned with the same amount of care that a dog takes wiping its arse.' *Itchy's review of a scummy bar, 2006*

'What?' You're thinking. 'You can't say that...' Oh yes we can. As the most straight talking-est, no-bullshit guide to going out in the UK, we'll never shy away from telling you if somewhere sucks harder than a toothless granny eating a boiled sweet. We also say nice things too.

Useful info

Useful info

TAXIS

Airline Licensed Private Hire
(0113) 244 4303

Euro Cabs
(0113) 244 8282

Express Cars
(0113) 278 0000

Holbeck Line
(0113) 243 3002

New Yellow Cars
(0113) 234 5666

Star Private Hire
(0113) 249 0099

BUSES

Arriva Yorkshire
(01924) 231 300

My Bus Metro
(0113) 348 1122

TRAINS

GNER Bookings
(08457) 722 225

Leeds City Railway Station
(0113) 245 2405

National Rail Enquiries
(08457) 484 950

TRAVEL INFORMATION

Metroline
(0113) 245 7676
Pretty much everything you need to know about bus and train services in Leeds.

Traveline
(08706) 082 608
www.traveline.org
Need to get from absolutely anywhere in Britain to absolutely anywhere else? Please call these guys as soon as possible.

PLANES

Leeds Bradford International Airport
(0113) 250 9696
This year, why not go somewhere a bit different for your hols, and visit wonderful Lbia? A truly modern town close to the city of Leeds, it has an ever expanding tourism industry providing jobs for the local Lbians. Ancient Lbia folklore has it that in the fields surrounding the town, there's a colony of giant flying beasts that must be given hundreds of human sacrifices each day.

TOURIST INFORMATION

Tourist Information
(0113) 242 5242
Clearly, we're your first port of call for information, but we have heard of situations involving tequila where people have, err, mislaid their Itchy guides. If that happens to you, you'll need to call tourist info to find out where to get another copy.

BEAUTY SALONS

The Beauty Crescent
12 The Crescent
(0113) 289 9122

Itchy is proud to crescent (ahem) the very finest Leeds' in beauty treatments. You'll feel like a right queen.

Mon–Sat, 10.30pm–6pm

Bliss Spa & Designer Nails
247 Otley Road
(0113) 230 4305

Remember a few years ago when Richard and Judy had someone go and get eyelash extensions? Well, they do that here, as well as everything else.

Mon–Wed, 9am–7pm;
Thu–Fri, 9am–8pm; Sat, 9am–6pm

Hanalee
Garden Unit, The Light, The Headrow
(0113) 244 9898

Our Fairy Godmother Hanalee transforms us into respectable ladies ready for the ball. Watch out Prince Charming, 'cos we're a coming to get ya.

Mon–Wed & Sat, 9am–6pm; Thu, 9am 'til late; Fri, 9am–7pm; Sun, 11am–5pm

Pamper and Polish
Mobile Beauty Service
(0790) 672 1135

The lovely Denise only sells two things, Nappies and the natives of Poland. Actually, if you ask nicely, she'll come to your house and do waxing, a facial, a tan or all sorts of things to do with nails.

By appointment

GYMS

LA Fitness
6–24 Albion Street
(0113) 243 3025

No, you used to be able to eat whatever. Not anymore. Oh dear.

Mon–Thu, 6.30am–10pm; Fri, 6.30am–8pm; Sat–Sun, 9am–5pm

Just Float
64 North Street
(0113) 243 3800

Take a break from all of the partying for one (half of a) night and, just float. You lie in a giant egg-shaped pod and feel gravity-free for one hour then brag about how refreshed and invigorated you feel.

Tue–Fri, 11am–8pm; Sat, 10am–4pm

Spirit Health & Fitness Club
Crowne Plaza Hotel, Wellingon Street
(0113) 261 6826

Burgers, pizzas and chinese + lager, vodka and wine = A, need to work out. Makeup, smoke and fake tan + partying, work stress and relationship woes = B, need to relax in a sauna. A + B = Spirit Health Club.

Mon–Sun, 7am–10pm

PERSONAL SHOPPING

Dressed
(07977) 184 624

Imagine having someone to tell you exactly what to wear everyday... and no, we don't mean your mum. If you're stuck for fashion ideas, these guys will help you get dressed.

By appointment

Useful info

TATTOO

Ace Art Tattoo Studio

75 Domestic Street, Holbeck

(0113) 245 8806

It doesn't look much from the outside, but let's be honest: if you're going to get some ink you might as well do it in a scary place.

🕒 *Times vary*

Physical Poetry Tattoo and Piercing

7a The Crescent, Hyde Park Corner

(0113) 225 0405

Two little Russian girls who sing squeaky songs in school girls outfits. Or beautifully created and personalized art, which should be shown at any opportunity.

🕒 *Mon–Sat, 12pm–6pm*

HAIRDRESSERS

Hair Cuttery

26 Arndale Centre

(0113) 274 4552

A drop-in hairdresser who'll sort you out faster than a speeding mullet, at the drop of a hat. And you won't need a hat afterwards.

🕒 *Mon–Sat, 9am–5.30pm*

Jeffrey Glass Hair Design

7 Burtons Arcade

(0113) 243 8905

Every girl knows that the best way to get over a break up is to change your hair. Chop it, feather it or spike it; just wash that man right out of your hair.

🕒 *Mon–Wed, 9am–6pm; Thu–Fri, 9am–7pm; Sat, 8.30am–5.30pm*

John Allen Hairdressing

129 High Street, Yeadon

(0113) 250 8002

Our straw poll says 97% of folk think your thatch looks like a haystack stuck to your scalp. Pitch in here, and fork out for a cut.

🕒 *Tue & Wed, 9am–6pm; Thu–Fri, 9am–7pm; Sat, 9am–5pm*

Toni & Guy

22 King Edward Street

(0113) 244 9610

Look, we're not being funny, but isn't it about time you all caught up with the fact that guys can have cool hair. Time to grow up and lose the 'angry hedge' look.

🕒 *Mon–Tue, 9am–5.15pm; Wed–Thu, 9am–6.45pm; Fri, 9am–6pm; Sat, 9am–5.15pm*

Box Creative Hairdressing

3 Lower Briggate

(0113) 245 6869

Haircuts can be nerve-wracking, but this boxing clever team ensure you leave looking like a page three stunner, not a tit. Their vast experience means they never make a boob of your barnet. Friendly stylists actually listen, and give honest advice about what will work. If you just want a trim they'll happily leave the hacking to the computer geeks, but they really excel in colours and restyles, with tons of ideas from subtle to traffic-stopping. If your locks resemble road kill through over-processing, the blissful conditioning treatments here will bring them back from the brink.

🕒 *Mon–Wed & Fri–Sat, 10am–6pm;*
Thu, 10am–7pm

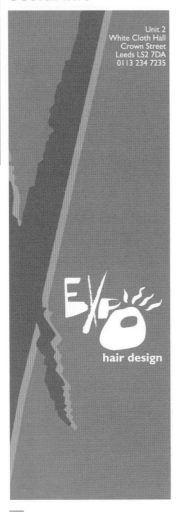

Unit 2
White Cloth Hall
Crown Street
Leeds LS2 7DA
0113 234 7235

Expo Hair Design
Unit 2, White Cloth Hall, Crown Street
(0113) 234 7235

Even if your crowning glory's got more splits than a gymnastics show, or your ponytail looks like an actual horse's bottom, Expo's excellent experts can save you. The care they take giving thorough consultations before each cut is truly outstanding, and with a heavenly mini head massage during washing, you'll be completely relaxed and reassured. As well as chopping barnets, they chop prices; cuts start at just £29, with 10% student discount on weekdays, and training sessions from 4pm on Mondays, when you can get snipped free or try colours from only a fiver.

© *Mon–Wed, Fri, 9am–6pm;*
Thu, 9am–7pm; Sat, 9am–5pm

LETTINGS AGENTS

Avtar Properties

127 Brudenell Road
(0113) 274 5111

LS6 a speciality; get toasty in the Chestnuts or choose from all manner of Manors. Whoever did the town planning in Leeds must be the laziest trout we've come across; they just thought of one name then stuck Avenue/Road/Street/ Place/Square etc. on the end of it. Consequently, finding the place you need when doing viewings can get confusing. Avtar's helpful blokeys can help stop you getting hassled in the Hessles or losing your head in the Headingleys.

🕒 *Jan–Easter, 9.30am–8pm;*
Easter–Jan, 9.30am–6pm

LS1 City Apartments

2 Cherry Tree Walk, The Calls
(0113) 234 4111
www.ls-1.co.uk

Should be called Elle-S1, as the prestige apartments this unique city centre specialist sells and rents are right out of a glossy mag. The great staff shine too. 'Life agents' really go the extra mile to help young professionals move to the busy, buzzy core of Leeds, with interior design services, mortgage advice, friendly, thorough consultations about what you need, and maintenance and housekeeping schemes to keep your dream pad polished. In fact, the only matt you'll find is the one saying 'Welcome' outside your new front door.

🕒 *Mon–Thu, 9am–6pm; Fri, 9am–5.30pm;*
Sat, 10am–4pm

Pickard Properties

172 Woodhouse Lane
(0113) 246 9395
www.pickardproperties.co.uk

The Pickard of the bunch, offering tons of extras. Itchy love that you can choose rent inclusive of bills (starting at just £65 per week) to help your budgeting, so you don't have to stay chilly because using any more gas than an amoeba's fart makes you worry about costs. Renewable energy resources are used for utilities wherever possible too. There are no signing fees, really helpful agents, and a 24-hour maintenance team ensuring you have a solid roof over your head, not falling onto it. This lot make the house hunting process smoother than Gillette.

🕒 *Call for an appointment*

Useful info

Park Lane Properties

25–27 Otley Road
(0113) 230 4949

Student-orientated letting company with many refurbished and renovated properties, so you're less likely to end up with a carpet that used to be plain beige but is now bright green. You know, one off those that looks like a furry Magic Eye and has the remains of a late night snack circa 1972 trodden into the pile. They also have a garden maintenance department, meaning bits of your property that are actually supposed to be bright green won't be beige. They'll ferry you about in one of their snazzy courtesy cars too; a great option if Leeds is raining more cats and dogs than you'd find in a cheap takeaway's freezer cabinet.

🕒 *Mon–Fri, 9am–5pm*

Redbrick Properties

48 Otley Road
(0113) 230 5552
www.redbrickproperties.co.uk

Exceedingly well red on the subject of renting in LS6. Check out their website for a wealth of useful info, including how to deal with condensation, which can be a pain in Leeds' otherwise gorgeous antique terraces. Their down-to-earth service is efficiently run, with properties maintained to a high standard and a reassuringly clear process for reporting any problems so they get fixed up and looking sharp quick-smart. Sure beats coming back to your mate's flea-ridden, saggy-breasted excuse for a sofa after another gruelling stint temping at the British Gas call centre.

🕒 *Mon–Fri, 9am–5.30pm; Sat, 10am–4pm*

Arabella insisted, that for the sake of her Prada shoes they had better move to the city.

It's not just your wardrobe that'll benefit from city living, in an über stylish LS1 apartment you'll be slap-bang in the centre of all that Leeds has to offer - cool bars, swanky restaurants, trendy shops, funky clubs and celeb spotting opportunities galore. Add to that world class cultural, sporting and music venues and there simply isn't a more vibrant place to live. So what are you waiting for? Come out of the middle of nowhere and into the middle of everything!

Just call one of our life agents on **0113 234 4111**; they're the most clued up 'movers and shakers' on the residential market.

LS¹ city apartments life agents, not just estate agents

sales & rentals **t 0113 234 4111** LS1, 2 cherry tree walk, the calls, leeds, LS2 7EB.
property management & id **t 0113 200 6350** LS1, magellan house, armouries way, clarence dock, leeds LS10 1JE.

e contact@one-uk.co.uk **www**.one-uk.co.uk

pickard

Raising the roof

HOME, HOME ON DERANGED – FINDING THE PERFECT PAD TO RENT IN LEEDS CAN BE A CRAZY AFFAIR. IF YOU'RE BRICKING IT ABOUT SOURCING DECENT DIGS THAT WILL SUIT YOUR STYLE AND YOUR BANK ACCOUNT, THEN FEAR NOT. ITCHY, IN ASSOCIATION WITH PICKARD PROPERTIES, TAKES YOU ON A WHISTLESTOP TOUR OF THE KEY STUDENT HOUSING AREAS, SO YOU CAN STOP BLEDDY WHISTLING AND ACTUALLY FIND SOMEWHERE TO SHACK UP

Headingley

The original Leeds student Mecca, and just like at the bingo, the cry is all too often 'full house'; if you want to sow your wild Hollyoats here you'll need to start pad hunting early on. Home to the cricket and rugby grounds, and more pubs and smart bars than old men have odd tufts of ear and nasal hair.

Hyde Park

If you're after retro hip and hippified, seek Hyde Park. Lay about in layered style – the artsy crowd here are all tassled fringing, sharp fringes, and Edinburgh Fringe. Chat literature in the wondrous LS6 café, then catch a flick at the cult Picture House before heading back to the 14 recycling bins jostling for space in your kitchen. The park becomes a mini festival ground in summer, packed with poi-twizzlers, frisbee chuckers and ice-cream vans playing *The A-Team* theme tune.

Woodhouse

You couldn't be closer to LU's Parky steps unless you camped there, so if you prefer to catch zeds than buses, this is the best place to live in the entire Uni-verse. Wrestle yourself from the duvet at the last possible minute and still make lectures on time, sporting the best funked up out-of-bed barnet bar none.

Burley

What's the difference between six and four? A helluva lot when it comes to postcodes and rent. Switch LS6 for LS4, and you'll still be only 15 minutes from Headingley shops, but with more in your pocket to spend there. Handily close to Burley Park railway station, Cardigan Fields leisure complex and the hallowed 24-hour Co-op too. You do the maths.

Horsforth

Turn city-dwelling mates green with envy by living somewhere with grass that hasn't sprouted under a heat lamp in someone's loft, yet has a growing nightlife. Live music at the Sand bar and hearty pub grub with proper tankard pints at the Severed Head mean the Hors is giving Headingley a good gallop for its money as a top spot to shack up.

Pickard can help you find a pad with absolutely no signing fees, a 24-hour maintenance team, and you can even have bills included in your rent if it helps you budget. Call (0113) 2469 395 or check out **www.pickardproperties.co.uk.**

Useful info

TAKEAWAY INDIAN

Indian Spice
19 Hyde Park Road
(0113) 244 9696
Delicious Indian food that comes in all shapes, sizes and flavours. They say variety is the spice of life, after all.
Mon–Sun, 2pm–12am

TAKEAWAY ITALIAN

La Besi
211 Clarendon Road, Hyde Park
(0113) 244 1177
You have to collect it, but it's always worth the jaunt. This is Italian soul food, the way Mamma used to make it.
Mon–Sat, 5pm–12am

TAKEAWAY ORIENTAL

Lucky Dragon
Templar Lane
(0113) 275 9913
You don't need a fortune cookie to tell you you're a very lucky dragon indeed to have food delivered from here.
Mon–Sat, 5pm–3.30am; Sun, 5pm–1am

Shanghai
70 Middleton Road
(0113) 253 3090
A Chinese restaurant that delivers in every sense of the word. Rumour has it that Madonna ate here once and was more than a little surprised to find Sean Penn sitting at the next table.
Mon–Sun, 5pm–3am

EVERYTHING ELSE

Flames
162b Woodhouse Lane
(0113) 245 3058
Balti, pizza, burgers, kebabs and chicken, all at once. A divine combination,don't you think? Especially at 3am. Plus, they deliver.
Mon–Sat, 5pm–3am; Sun, 5pm–1am

Pizza Hut
33 Briggate
(0113) 244 8701
A decent slice at a decent price. This is the daddy when it comes to massive bits of dough, laced with great big gooey strings of lovely cheese.
Mon–Thu, 11am–9pm; Fri–Sat, 11am–10pm; Sun, 12pm–9pm

Support

Illustration by Joly Braime

Police (non-emergency)

Call this number to report an incident, or if police presence is required less urgently.
(0845) 606 0606

Samaritans

93 Clarendon Road
(0113) 245 6789
www.samaritans.org.uk

NHS Direct (24 hour help and advice)

0845 4647
www.nhsdirect.nhs.uk

Leeds General Infirmary

Great George Street
(0113) 243 2799
www.leedsteachinghospitals.com

Family Planning

28 Kirkgate
(0113) 3057 884

Leeds Centre for Sexual Health

Sunnybank Wing, Leeds General Infirmary
0113) 392 6762

Rape Helpline

(0113) 224 0058

Fire and Rescue - Leeds Fire Station

Kirkstall Road
(0113) 244 0855

Samaritans

93 Clarendon Road
(0113) 245 6789

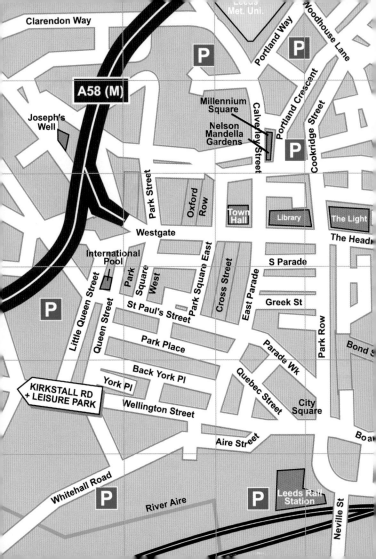

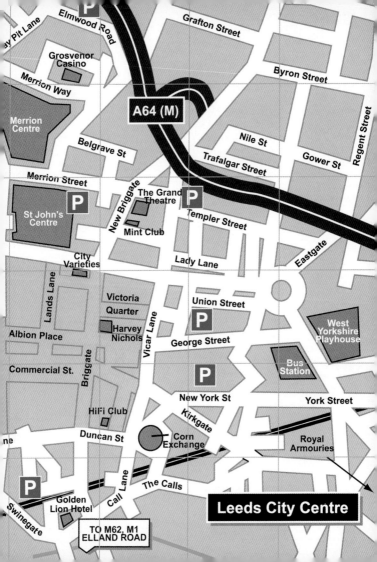

Leeds City Centre

Index

Index

Index